PLANES and PILOTS

HAWKER
HURRICANE
from 1935 to 1945

Dominique BREFFORT

Color profiles by Nicolas GOHIN
Translated from the French by Alan McKay

Histoire & Collections

Above.
The Hurricane prototype (K5083) in flight during its initial trials at the beginning of 1936, with serial number and roundels but not yet armed. (Hawker)

FROM THE "MONOPLANE INTERCEPTOR" TO THE HURRICANE

ALTHOUGH THE FIRST BRITISH COMBAT PLANE to fly faster than 300 mph, produced almost to the end of World War II and used on every front, the Hawker Hurricane hasn't always been recognised for what it was worth because although its career was brilliant it was to a great extent eclipsed by that of the true star, the Supermarine Spitfire. The real winner of the Battle of Britain however was the Hurricane, and by far, since in the summer of 1940 two thirds of RAF Fighter Command's squadrons were equipped with Hurricanes. Even better, at the end of the war, the Hurricane had chalked up a very impressive tally, since more than half of all British kills, all theatres of operations included, were scored by the different versions of the Hurricanes.

From biplane to monoplane

At the very beginning of the thirties, the biplane fighter reigned supreme in all the modern air forces; although the concept dated back to the Great War, there seemed to be no need to question it, either in France or Germany or of course in Great Britain. Moreover at the time ever since 1929, this lack of innovation was aggravated by the serious economic crisis which all the western countries were going through and which literally stifled all research and official orders. In England for example, Fighter Command consisted of thirteen squadrons, of which eight were equipped with British Bulldogs, three with Hawker Furies and two with Hawker Demons. All these planes were derived from machines built during WWI and shared the same armament – a pair of fuselage-mounted Vickers machine guns, in front of the pilot so that he could rearm them easily, a necessary precaution for weapons which tended to jam easily. Attitudes changed at RAF headquarters when Lord Trenchard was replaced. Trenchard was a fierce supporter of General Douhet's theories – the pre-eminence of the bomber over the fighter – but was replaced by Sir John Salmond in January 1930. Salmond was aware that it was absolutely vital to modernise and reinforce British fighters, particularly when faced with the growing threats coming from Europe. He was behind Specification F.7/30 brought out the same year for a new fighter made mainly of metal, able to reach 250 mph – a speed considered to be the maximum for a biplane at the time – and armed with at least four machine guns. The tender was intended to replace the main RAF fighter, the Bulldog (the better performing Fury was only reserved for three elite squadrons), and was won by the Gloster Gladiator which thus became the last RAF biplane fighter and whose career lasted until the first years of the war, particularly in the Mediterranean and Middle East theatres.

At the same time, talented young designers working for European aircraft builders decided to break away from twenty-year-old theories and devoted themselves to studying the only design which according to them would be able to yield really high performances: a monoplane fighter. At Hawker's[1], whose design team was led by Sidney Camm[2], the starting point was in fact the Fury which became the last fighter biplane the company made and was an aircraft which, when it came out, was a sort of apogee of aviation concepts.

The first step in conceiving the future machine, called simply "Fury Monoplane", was to design a low cantilever-type wing, built around two main longerons and covered with fabric. The 660 bhp Rolls Royce Goshawk was chosen as its powerplant, but as the engine's complicated cooling system made it vulnerable, it was quickly decided to replace it with another engine, one that the engine builder was working on at his own expense, the PV 12, when it was finally ready in January 1934. In order to assert the resolutely modern side of the fighter, it had an entirely closed-in cockpit – a rare thing at the time – as well as retractable undercarriage. As for armament, this had to be reinforced since it was thought that because of the new machine's high speed, the pilot would only have a very short time to aim at the target in and that a heavy concentration of fire would therefore make up for this disadvantage.

The project started officially at Hawker's in 1933 and very quickly differed so much from the original Fury that in May the following year, the firm's design team, established at Kingston, decided to call it the "Interceptor Monoplane". With better performances being possible with Rolls Royce's two-stage supercharged PV 12 delivering 60% more power, compared with the Kestrel then available, Camm literally designed his machine around the powerplant. As for the intended armament, according to Specification F.4/34, this consisted of four Colt Browning .303 machine guns; the licence to produce them in Great Britain had been requested by the Armament Research Division at the beginning of 1934; this specification was modified in September the following year and almost adapted to match the Hawker plane (Specification F.36/34) with the armament increased to six or eight guns of the same calibre.

Hawker's Interceptor Monoplane was brought out on 4 September 1934 and presented to the authorities who accepted it, with a scale 1 model being made before the end of the same year armed with four machine guns, two Vickers in the fuselage and two others – or two Brownings – in the wings. The plane was built with a low cantilever wing, made up of a central section which was interdependent of the fuselage, and two outer parts with a decreasing cross-section. This wing was entirely fabric covered except for the leading edges, which were made of metal; it comprised caissons which housed the machine guns firing outside the propeller arc, thus getting round the need to fit any synchronisation. The structure of the fuselage was characteristic of Hawker's previous creations, with a rectangular assembly of steel tubes completed by formers and wooden stiffeners, this latticework offering both strength and lightness. The outer rounded form of the fuselage was obtained by the wooden and canvas skin (at the rear) and by Duralumin

Opposite.
Sir Sydney Camm (1893-1966), the "father" of the Hurricane. Appointed Chief Engineer at Hawker's in 1923, he contributed to the making of, among others, the Hart and Fury biplanes before designing the Tempest, Typhoon, Hunter as well as the P1127 which gave rise to the VTOL Harrier.

Opposite.
The Hawker Fury was the direct forebear of the Hurricane. This biplane's performances were very good and it was reserved for the elite squadrons. Here planes from No17 Squadron bearing hastily applied roundels and camouflage after the Munich Crisis in 1938.

Below.
Before the Hurricane arrived, the Bristol Bulldog was the most numerous plane in RAF Fighter Command.

This page.
The Hurricane prototype was slightly different from the production series machines: tail plane struts (suppressed during the trials but its armament was fitted), canopy, engine cowling, undercarriage doors and exhaust pipes. All the metal parts, particular the front of the aircraft, were polished while the fabric-covered parts were painted aluminium, which explains why the shades are different. (Hawker)

(at the front, especially for the engine cowlings). The cockpit was covered entirely by a rearwards sliding canopy which could be jettisoned in emergencies. The undercarriage had a wide track leaving enough room for the large radiator which was essential for cooling the engine; it was also fitted with low-pressure tyres; it was retractable as was the tail-wheel and was equipped with hydraulic brakes. Once this model had been presented officially, it was decided by modifying the initial Specification F.63/34, to arm the future machine, for which Sydney Camm envisaged a top speed of 331.25 mph (530kph) at 15 580 ft (4 570 m), with eight Colt-Browning machine guns just as soon as the licence to produce them was obtained (by BSA).

On 21 February 1935, an official contract for the production of a prototype was signed; it was given the military serial number "K5083". The following August, the airframe was completed and was fitted with its engine at the end of the same month. The engine, at first called the PV 12, was renamed Merlin and the variant intended for Specification F.36/34, "Merlin C", rated at 1 025 bhp on take off and driving a wooden two-bladed Watts propeller, enabling this prototype to reach 270 mph at sea-level, 315 mph at 16 200 ft and 235 mph at 30 000 ft, with the service ceiling being fixed at 35 400 ft and the rate of climb at 2 400 ft per minute.

On 23 October 1935, K5083 was conveyed by road to Brooklands and after a few taxiing trials and engine run-ups, it took to the air for the first time on 6 November 1935, flown by Flight-Lieu-

These two photos taken at the Hawker factory in 1938 give a very good idea of how the Hurricane was designed with in particular a fuselage consisting of a fabric-covered alloy-tubing framework. (Hawker)

rwent some modifications, the tail-plane struts being suppressed, the canopy and the windshield redesigned and the undercarriage doors modified and simplified[3].

At the beginning of 1937, the series of trials was interrupted briefly when it was decided to replace the original engine, which had had a few problems. The Merlin F (or Mk I) with which it was originally intended to be fitted had been reserved for the Fairey Battle bomber; in the end it was the Merlin G (or Mk II) rated at 1 030 bhp which was chosen to equip the production series examples. The new engine being different, mainly where the mountings were concerned, the forward part of the fuselage had to be considerably redesigned, delaying series production by a few weeks.

Apart from these almost inevitable teething problems which did not cast any doubt on the aircraft's safety, the authorities considered the prototype to be overall fit for service without any major defect. At the end of the trials, the prototype was also used for various tests before finishing its career as a ground training airframe.

At the end of this series of trials, the A & AEE reported favourably to the Air Ministry which ordered 600 machines from Hawker's on 3 June 1936 and officially called the new plane the "Hurricane" on the 27 of the same month. This order, the biggest ever placed since the end of the Great War and unheard of in peacetime, did not however inconvenience the aircraft manufacturer who had already taken the initiative – the new chairman Thomas Sopwith having decided with the agreement of his board a month earlier – to launch the production of 1 000 Hurricanes at the Brooklands and Kingston factories without waiting for the official decision, so sure was he of his fighter's success!

The first production series Hurricane (serial number L1547) flew for the first time on 12 October 1937 at the airfield near the Brooklands factory, with Philip Lucas at the controls. Less than a month later, four machines had already taken to the air. These differed from the prototype by their three exhaust pipes (instead of six previously) located along each side of the cowling, and the different shape of the forward part of the fuselage with notably the appearance of a boss on the front over the first exhaust pipe, a modification caused by fitting the Merlin II engine. The canopy was modified: the windshield without uprights was fitted with a flat pane on the front part, the tail-wheel was now fixed and a landing light had been fitted in the left wing leading edge. These planes' maximum speed was 320 mph at 15 600 ft and they were fitted with Watts Z.28 wooden constant-pitch two-bladed propellers.

tenant Paul "George" Bulman. On landing after a flawless flight, the pilot made this rather curt comment to Camm, summarising the aircraft's qualities: "Another winner, I think." As the story goes, four months earlier, the plane which became the future Hurricane's main adversary, the Messerschmitt Bf 109, had also taken to the air…

From prototype to production series

Sent to the A & AEE (Aeroplane and Armament Experimental Establishment) at Martlesham Heath on 7 February 1936 for a series of trials, this time official ones, carried out by Sergeant "Sammy" Wroath, the prototype exceeded 312.5 mph (500 kph), easily faster than the original specification required. Having been fitted with its weapons in July 1936, the prototype unde-

---

1. The H.G. Hawker Engineering Company had replaced Sopwith's in 1920; it subsequently became the Hawker Aircraft Company.
2. Sidney Camm had been the Chief Designer at Hawker's since 1925. In the same year he had already imagined a monoplane fighter powered by a Jupiter engine.
3. The undercarriage well doors were originally in two parts, the lower one being movable. This system was thought to be too complicated and was modified and simplified, the lower part of the wheel finally being left uncovered, without the lower door to cover it.

*Above.
A group of Mk Is from No 73 Squadron, NO67 Wing AASF in flight over France just before the Blitzkrieg. The planes, equipped with three-bladed propellers, had their fins painted à la Française, most of them having also had their fuselage codes reduced to the individual number only, to avoid any possible confusion. (IWM)*

HURRICANE MARK I

THE FIRST SQUADRON to be equipped with the new fighter was No 111 at Northolt just before Christmas 1937, followed by No 3 at Kenley then by No 56 in the following six months, so that by the end of 1938 two hundred Hurricanes had been delivered to Fighter Command. When it was put into service, the Hurricane became the first RAF fighter to reach 300 mph but it was also the first British monoplane interceptor with a closed cockpit and retractable undercarriage. The pilots had to get used to this machine which literally went against all the practices that had been in vogue till then, with this conversion being rather delicate since at the time the Hurricane was introduced there were no other aircraft with comparable performances which could be used for training.

Whilst it was being put into operation, further trials carried out mainly in the wind tunnel showed that in certain flying conditions, especially under a high stall rate, the plane took a considerable amount of time to get out of a spin and that it was therefore necessary to change the flow of air over the lower surfaces. For this a "keel" was added to the rear of the fuselage from the sixty-first production series machine onwards and the not very effective rudder was enlarged slightly at its base.

Entering service and more improvements

At the time of the Munich Crisis, in September 1938, Fighter Command put its squadrons on alert but out of the twelve official Hurricane units at that time, only two, Nos 56 and 111, were actually operational whilst only a handful of Spitfires was operational in No 19 Squadron at Duxford. Faced with this situation, Hawker was asked to increase its fighter production rate no matter what the cost, if needs be getting the production lines to operate night and day.

The result was not long in coming and in October 1938, production was high enough to re-equip one squadron per month and at the same time make up losses and replace machines already in service with new, modified ones since thirty machines were coming off the production lines at the Brooklands factory every month by the end of the same year.

All the machines produced up until then were powered by the Merlin II driving a Watts wooden two-bladed propeller and trials were carried out on the sixteenth production series machine to find a replacement propeller. Two models were tried out one after the other; first the de Havilland designed three-bladed two-pitch propeller, the Hydromatic – in fact the Hamilton Standard made under licence in Great Britain – which considerably improved take off performance and landing and which began to be fitted on production series aircraft at the end of 1938. There was also a constant speed model, the Rotol (short for Rolls-Royce and Bristol), which also had three blades, fitted with a Spitfire-type propeller boss driven by a new version of the Merlin, the Mk III rated at 1 030 bhp on take off and especially equipped with a hydraulic pressure variation system enabling the pitch to be changed automatically, as well as a "universal" prop shaft, enabling it in the future to take any propeller.

With this new engine-propeller combination, the Hurricane's performances improved greatly, especially its rate of climb, due to the propeller pitch and power being adapted to the altitude, and the engine not over-revving when diving. The first plane equipped with the new Rotol propeller flew on 24 January 1939; this was L1877, modified and specially painted aluminium, which reached 334 mph at 15 000 feet. Subsequently this machine was used for testing further variants of the Rotol propeller or the Merlin engine.

The other improvement concerned the wings themselves, which Hawker's had already studied at the beginning of 1938.

Above.
No85 Squadron Hurricanes on their French base at the beginning of 1940. This unit was part of the Advanced Air Striking Force which also included some Fairey Battles and Bristol Blenheims which the Hurricanes had to protect. (IWM)

In order to reinforce them, metal skin replaced the fabric used on the early production models. On the other hand the fabric covering the fuselage and the moving surfaces was not changed and was even retained until the plane's production lines ceased in 1944.

It was decided to introduce the new metal wing originally designed to house eight machine guns, in the summer of 1939 following conclusive trials, also on L1877. As it was clearly stipulated that this improvement was not to perturb the fighter production rate (800 examples ordered in 1938, followed by 1 700 machines to be produced by Gloster), there followed a rather unlikely situation in which a large number of planes fitted with the old wing continued to be built, whilst in parallel, metal wings were also being produced and waiting to be fitted; fitting them took three hours. This explains why in 1940, a number of operational units still flew planes with fabric covered wings while the metal wings they were supposed to be fitted with were stocked in the factories or the maintenance centres.

Apart from the metal wing which was "retro"-fitted on older examples during maintenance and new Merlin III engines driving the Rotol propeller, the end of series Hurricane Mk Is (sometimes mistakenly called Mk IA) had increased protection (armoured windshield and armoured plate fitted in front of the cockpit), and deflection sights linked to external pointers. Other trials were also carried out in 1939 with regard to the Hurricane's "tropicalisation" by installing a dust filter in front of the carburettor air intake housed in a fairing under the nose, a modification done to machines which were to be deployed overseas [1].

Moreover, in order to increase the plane's firepower, a Hurricane was fitted with two 20-mm Oerlikon cannon, which were quickly replaced by a pair of easier-to-operate and more reliable 20-mm Hispano Mk Is.

The high Hurricane production rate was kept up all during 1939 so much so that in April 300 machines had been built, equipping thirteen squadrons [2]. This rate at one time exceeded the speed at which pilots could convert to the new fighter.

On the eve of WWII, in the summer of 1939, a large part of the RAF day-fighter units were equipped with monoplanes, the Hurricane having the lion's share compared with the more modern and faster Spitfire, equipping as it did sixteen squadrons, with another in the process of being formed.

Opposite.
Hurricane L1648 was one of the Mark I series and was distinguishable by its Watts three-bladed propeller, its fabric covered wings and no ridge under the fuselage. Assigned to No 85 Squadron, this plane crashed on landing at Debden on 16 October 1938 and was written-off. (Hawker)

1. A conflict with Italy was envisaged in North Africa (Cyrenaica) after Munich.
2. Nos 1, 3, 32, 43, 46, 56, 73, 79, 85, 87, 111, 151 and 213 together with two Auxiliary Air Force squadrons, No 501 and 504.

A line up of No 111 Squadron Hurricane Mk Is from the beginning of the series. This unit's markings are non-regulation: the number 111 on the fuselage in place of the usual code is painted the flight's colour.

Out of the 572 planes coming off the production lines before 1 September 1939, 280 were in their units (most of them however were from the beginning of production, with fabric covered wings and Merlin II engines), 133 were in the workshops or being used for trials, the remaining 169 examples were either intended for export or destroyed, or being repaired after an accident. Thus the target stipulated in the contract of having 600 machines ready had been met when war broke out.

The Phoney War and the Fall of France

On 1 September 1939, RAF Fighter Command could line up, apart from its sixteen Hurricane squadrons, seven other totally operational units equipped with Spitfires, five with twin-engined Blenheim Mk Is and four biplane squadrons – three with Gladiators and one with Gauntlets. As can be seen Fighter Command's Boss Sir Hugh Dowding's initial target of fifty-two fighter squadrons was far from being approached, let alone met.

Very soon after war was declared, four Hurricane squadrons were sent to France, two of which (Nos 1 and 73) formed the Air Component part of the British Expeditionary Force (BEF) which set itself up on the Belgian border, while the other two (Nos 85 and 87) were part of the Advanced Air Striking Force (AASF) which also included some light Battle and Blenheim bombers which they were given the task of protecting.

British involvement was evidently deliberately limited, to the great displeasure of the French who would have liked to see their allies committing themselves further, but Dowding thought – though without ever saying so officially – that there was no point putting his precious fighters in danger if the situation on the front did not require them.

During what was called the Phoney War, air activity was limited – on both sides – to recce missions, or even some bombing operations but only involved a limited number of aircraft. Nonetheless some occasionally rougher clashes took place during this seemingly quiet period, the first British kill being scored when a Hurricane from No 1 Squadron shot down a Dornier Do 17P over Toul on 30 October 1939.

It was also at this time that the new models of Hurricane were delivered to the operational units, priority being given to replacing the aircraft still equipped with the Merlin II and Watts two-bladed propellers now deployed in France.

On 10 May 1940, the Germans launched their lightning attack on Holland, Luxemburg, Belgium and France with the intention of going round the Maginot Line and rushing to the Channel in order to cut off the British Expeditionary Force and divide the French forces. At that moment the Air Component of the BEF and the AASF numbered less than one hundred Hurricanes. Nos 607 and 615 Squadrons were right in the middle of converting and still had a dozen or so Gladiators in their ranks when they were added to the four squadrons already deployed in September 1939. As soon as he learnt of the German attack, Dowding ordered four extra

SPECIFICATIONS HURRICANE MARK I

Type: Single seat fighter
Powerplant
One Rolls Royce Merlin II or III, liquid-cooled, supercharged V-12 engine, rated at 1 030 bhp and driving, depending on the examples, a Watts two-blade constant pitch propeller, or a de Havilland-Hamilton three-blade metal propeller, or even a three-blade constant speed Rotol propeller.
Dimensions
Length: 31 ft 5 in (9,58 m)
Height: 13 ft 1 in (3,99 m)
Wingspan: 40 ft (12,19 m)
Wing Surface: 257.990 sq ft (23,97 m²)
Weight (empty): 4 569 lb (2 118 kg)
Weight (fully laden): 6 586 lb (2 994 kg)
Performance
Maximum speed: 320 mph (512 km/h)
Maximum range: 443 miles (708 km)
Operational Ceiling: 33 390 ft (10 180 m)
Armament
Eight wing-mounted 7.7-mm (.303-in) Browning machine guns with 2 600 rounds.
Production
1 994 examples built by Hawker Aircraft Ltd, 1 850 by Gloster Aircraft C° Ltd and 380 by Canadian Car and Foundry Corporation, under licence. Total: 4 224 Mk I.

Above.
A simulated gas attack on No 87 Squadron's airfield at Lille-Seclin in France at the beginning of 1940. At the time, the unit's insignia was (partly) painted on the tail fin and the underwing surfaces were painted white on the right and black on the left. (IWM)

squadrons to be sent, Nos 3, 79 and 504 to reinforce the Air Component and No 501 to support the AASF.

The fighting in May and June 1940 was particularly hard on Fighter Command units on the Continent and it is thought that, after the troops were evacuated from Dunkirk (Operation Dynamo) on 4 June, some 30% of the planes and 20% of the pilots committed had been lost[3]. Britain was not long in calling its units back home, especially to defend the homeland against the invasion that was thought to be both imminent and inevitable, so much so that by 18 June 1940, all the squadrons were back across the Channel[4] in England, which was where all operations over the continent would start.

As the Campaign for France was in full swing, one RAF squadron (No 46) was sent to Norway on 26 May 1940, six weeks after the Germans had invaded the country. Transported by sea to Skaaland in order to protect the Allied troops fighting to protect the port at Narvik, the unit fought successfully against the Luftwaffe, scoring thirty or so kills before being called back to Britain. Ordered at first to destroy their planes where they were, the squadron finally decided to leave with its aircraft, so as not to weaken the Home defence forces which were sorely in need of aircraft at the time. Thus ten surviving Hurricanes managed to deck land on the aircraft carrier HMS Glorious that had brought them to Norway, doing so without the necessary landing equipment and in spite of the pilots' lack of experience. Unfortunately this exploit was reduced to nothing a few days later when the ship was sunk on its way back and all the planes and their pilots, but two, were lost.

During the French Campaign, the Hurricane nonetheless confirmed the good impression it had given during its first trials, namely that it was a very good gun platform, that it was stable and robust and that its wide undercarriage track enabled it to use very hastily prepared airstrips. When confronting its main rival, the Bf 109, it had proved that it was both more manoeuvrable and better armed, with the German fighter being much faster, particularly in a dive thanks to is engine fitted with fuel injection. Thus although an "Emil" could always get out of a scrap with its speed, the Hurricane could also almost always get out, while the going was still good, if it managed to engage its adversary in a dogfight where its manoeuvrability would make all the difference.

The Hurricane pilots had thereby caused the Luftwaffe quite heavy losses, successes which would be important in the fighting to come. Between 10 and 21 May, i.e. during the heaviest fighting, the Hurricane units alone claimed 499 confirmed kills and 123 probables, claims which were very often exaggerated since the Germans admitted to losing 299 machines for the same period to which they added 65 others which were too seriously damaged to be repaired. The most efficient unit in the AASF was No 1 Squadron which, as the story goes, had scored the first kill of the war, with 63 kills; this was nonetheless just beaten by No 3 Squadron (from the Air Component) with 67 kills.

In fact as was often the case, all these successes were the work of a limited number of pilots; 41 of them earned the title "ace" (at least five confirmed kills) during the French Campaign with the highest scorer being Fl. Off. Leslie Clishy, from No 1 Squadron (16 kills and one shared) who also had the sad privilege of being one of three Hurricane aces shot down during the Blitzkrieg...

The real winner of the Battle of Britain

Although the Luftwaffe came out of the French Campaign victorious, it had nonetheless been severely mauled, the six weeks'

---

3. 135 Spitfires, Hurricanes, Blenheims and Defiants were lost and 84 pilots killed or listed as missing just for Operation Dynamo. For the RAF, total losses for the Blitzkrieg amounted to 949 planes of which 386 were Hurricanes (out of a total of 477 fighters shot down during the period) and almost 200 pilots killed, seriously wounded or missing.
4. No 1, without planes was evacuated by boat from St Nazaire and No 73 set fire to all its planes before embarking at St Malo; only No 501, the last squadron still present in France and which had been ordered to protect the evacuation of the last BEF elements from Cherbourg, returned to Great Britain with its Hurricanes (eight of them...) after transiting via the Channel Islands.

Two Hurricane Mk Is from No 615 (County of Surrey) Squadron, Northolt, October 1940. Fourteen FAFL (Free French) pilots, including the famous René Mouchotte, were incorporated into this squadron at the end of the Battle of Britain. (IWM)

fighting having turned out to be much fiercer than the Germans had expected, due particularly to the opposition put up by the Armée de l'Air and its ally, the RAF. This was why the assault on Great Britain, which both sides considered to be inevitable, did not begin immediately, a pause of one month being observed enabling the Germans and the British to tend their wounds and build up their strength before the final assault and the planned invasion of England (Operation Seelöwe – Sea Lion).

For this, the Luftwaffe concentrated 2 500 planes, of which more than 1 600 were bombers, on its new bases ranging from Northern France to Norway, the first objective being to destroy the RAF in order to gain air superiority. On the other side, the RAF could field slightly more than 800 fighters, of which more than 500 were Hurricanes, shared out among 29 squadrons.

The Battle of Britain as it came to be called, started "officially" on 10 July 1940[5] with the Luftwaffe attacking Channel convoys following several operations intended to test the British defences. Fighter Command's strategy on this occasion was very simple and had been set up before the war. It consisted of using its two principal fighters according to their respective capabilities: the Spitfire which was faster and better at altitude, was to attack the escorting Bf 109s whilst the Hurricane, flying lower down was given the job of destroying the bombers flying at medium altitude. During these initial clashes over the Channel, the RAF units lost on average one fighter for three or four Luftwaffe aircraft, with the Hurricane, being more numerous, suffering higher losses.

The fighting intensified on Adlertag (Eagle Day) on 10 August when the Luftwaffe directly attacked British airfields and strategic military installations; these were sizeable operations, intended to pave the way for the landing planned for mid-September.

This first phase of the battle was intended, according to Goering, the all-powerful boss of the Luftwaffe, to shoot the RAF out of the skies in four days, but turned out to be a failure with the RAF squadrons, theoretically outnumbered by the enemy, managing to inflict heavy losses on their opponents in particular the Stuka or Bf 110 Gruppen, some of which were literally wiped out. Losses on the English side however were also heavy, with Fighter Command on several occasions having to launch virtually all its available strength, leaving no reserves.

Faced with this unexpected setback, the Luftwaffe changed its strategy and decided at the beginning of September to attack the major British towns. Although this second phase, known as the Blitz, ended up causing a lot of civilian casualties and the almost total destruction of some cities, it did loosen the stranglehold on Fighter Command, allowing it to rebuild its severely tried and weakened forces.

The first raid against London took place on 7 September and was one of the greatest air battles of WWII involving 1 250 machines fighting in a relatively restricted air space - some 37 miles long by barely 6 miles wide. At the end of this fighting, one hundred aircraft were strewn all over Southern England; 59 of them belonged to the Luftwaffe, and 29 were Hurricanes. However, in spite of these not negligible losses, the wheel of fortune was starting to turn in favour of the RAF and Great Britain.

Indeed following a massive raid against London on 15 September and which was a serious setback for the Luftwaffe, German headquarters, with Hitler at its head, decided that invading England from the sea would not be possible as long as Fighter Command had not been put out of action. These air raids continued nonetheless for several weeks, some on the same large scale as that on 27 September against the Bristol factory at Filton, in which the Luftwaffe lost 54 aircraft against 18 Spitfires and 10 Hurricanes shot down and fifteen English pilots killed.

Despite being reinforced by an Italian expeditionary corps based in Belgium, the rate of enemy operations against the British Isles dropped considerably in October, with the Luftwaffe beginning to use its Bf 109s as fighter-bombers (Jagdbombers or Jabos)) and the air raids becoming rarer and rarer with the approach of winter and the bad weather.

At the end of the Battle of Britain, the Germans had lost more than 1 600 aircraft (of which more than 500 were Messerschmitt Bf 109s) against a little more than 800 Spitfires and Hurricanes on the English side. Hawker's fighter, which was the most numerous during the three months of fighting, had again proved how capable it was, scoring more than half Fighter Command's kills recorded for that period; its availability during this same period was exceptional thanks to its sturdiness with more than 60% of planes damaged during the Battle of Britain being put back into service after being repaired. This was due especially to the shadow factories – delocalised, camouflaged factories set up by the Air Ministry in July 1940. Even better, two thirds of all Hurricanes put into the line were new and the remainder were aircraft which had been repaired.

Because of its easy maintenance and flying qualities, the Hurricane enabled a large number of foreign pilots (Czechs, Poles, Americans, Belgians and French) to take part in the fighting; this fighter was allocated to them as a priority mainly because it was

---

5. The "Battle of Britain" clasp of the WWII medal was awarded to any Fighter Command pilots who had fought between this date and 31 October, the official date of the end of the Battle of Britain even if 8 August is also evoked as being the start of the fighting.

Above.
Two Hurricane MK Is from No 501 (County of Gloucester) Squadron take off from their Rockford base on 15 August 1940 during the first phase of the Battle of Britain. These two planes were shot down by the same pilot, Oberleutnant Schoepfel of III./JG 26 "Schlageter" three days later… (IWM)

available in greater numbers than the Spitfire which was admittedly more sought after and more prestigious, but also available in fewer numbers and not so easy to handle. Later the situation changed because at the end of 1940, Spitfire production had increased to such an extent that all squadrons could be equipped with this fighter, which thanks to its all metal construction turned out to be faster to produce than the wood and fabric Hurricane.

First export sales

Despite the priority given to RAF orders, Hawker was able to organise its production lines just before the war started in such a way as to satisfy a few foreign customers, the British authorities having given the go-ahead for the new fighter to be delivered to "friendly" countries, those likely to oppose Nazi Germany. Yugoslavia had evaluated the machine in 1938 at first and ordered twelve then a further twelve in February 1940; 40 were to have been produced under licence by Rogozarski in Belgrade and sixty at Zmaj. Poland had also ordered some Hurricanes but in the end it only received one machine before the war started. Apart from Rumania (twelve examples were being delivered when the war started), Turkey (15 Mk Is), Persia (two examples in 1939-1940) and South Africa (three planes delivered to No 1 Squadron in Pretoria in December 1938), in the end it was Belgium (twenty examples delivered by Hawker in 1939 and a further eighty to be built by Fairey) and Finland (11 former RAF planes delivered at the end of the Winter War) which were the first to use the Hurricane in combat after Great Britain – with varying degrees of success, as will be seen in another chapter.

The end of an honourable career

The real winner of the Battle of Britain because it scored half the recorded kills for the period, AA included, the Hurricane Mk I, Fighter Command's most numerous fighter in the summer of 1940 with almost two thirds of its strength engaged[6], started to be replaced gradually in front-line squadrons by a more effective version, the Mk II equipped with the Merlin XX (see following chapter). Used for training missions at first, the Mk Is were to be seen again in combat but this time overseas especially in the Western Desert, or on Malta which was being continually attacked ever since Italy had entered the war in June 1940 and where No 261 Squadron was transferred during the height of the Battle of Britain.

Before the end of the year, three squadrons (Nos 33, 73 and 274) were equipped with "tropicalised" Hurricane Is equipped with Vokes filters which reduced its performance slightly (top speed: 312 mph). These aircraft served in the Mediterranean theatre until the end of 1941 with No 33 Squadron, commanded by the RAF's ace of aces, Squadron Leader Marmaduke T. St John Pattle, being sent to Greece then to Crete to cover the retreating British troops.[7]

---

6. 1 715 Hurricanes took part in the Battle of Britain and were credited with 1 792 kills (1 593 according to other sources) or 80% of the total score (2 739 claims).
7. At the time of his death on 19 April 1941, Pattle was without doubt the highest scoring Allied air ace with at least thirty kills to its credit in less than nine month's operations.

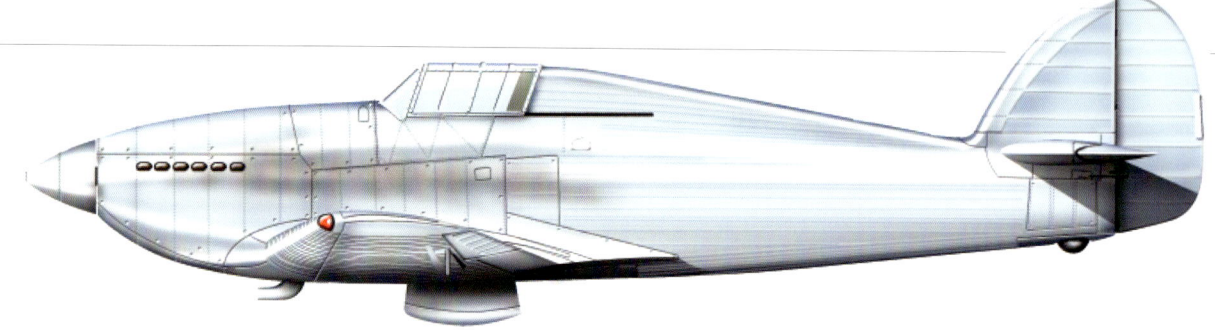

The prototype of the Hawker Hurricane (serial number K5083) made its maiden flight at Brooklands on 6 November 1935. It took part in a whole series of trials, was fitted with different versions of the Merlin engine and its armament was installed in August 1936. In September of the following year it took part in the film "Shadow of the Wing". It is shown here at the beginning of its career without markings or roundels, the fabric covered parts painted aluminium and those made of metal carefully polished.

Hawker Hurricane Mark I (L1679) from No 1 Squadron, Berry-au-Bac (France), May 1940, Pilot: Flight Officer Paul Richey. As part of the Advanced Air Striking Force (AASF) deployed in France after the outbreak of war, No 1 Squadron claimed a hundred or so kills during its stay on the Continent for the loss of 17 Hurricanes and two pilots. The underside of this plane which was from the beginning of the series and had fabric covered wings and wooden two-bladed propeller, was painted light blue in the field.

Hawker Hurricane Mk I (P3395) from No 1 Squadron, Collyweston, England, November 1940. The wasp painted on both sides of this plane's cowling was the pilot's personal insignia: Flight Officer A. V. Clowes added a stripe to the body for each kill. Clowes obtained a final tally of nine confirmed kills of which one was shared.

Hawker Hurricane Mk I (L1975) from No 17 Squadron, Debden, England, 1939. This plane bears the camouflage and the characteristic markings from the beginning of 1939 with fuselage roundels changed to "Type A" (tricolour), the under sides painted partly aluminium and black, over which the serial number was painted in large figures and the unit insignia on the tail covered with black ("Special Night").

Hawker Hurricane Mk I (N2359) from No 17 Squadron, Debden, England, June 1940. The Type A fuselage roundel with yellow edge (here the large version) was introduced in June 1940 whereas No 17 Sqn was given a new unit code ("YB" instead of "UV") at the outbreak of war in September 1939. Aboard this plane decorated with a personal insignia showing a winged Popeye (something rare in the RAF at the time), the Czech pilot Frantisek Fajtl shot down a Dornier Do 215 on 24 October 1940.

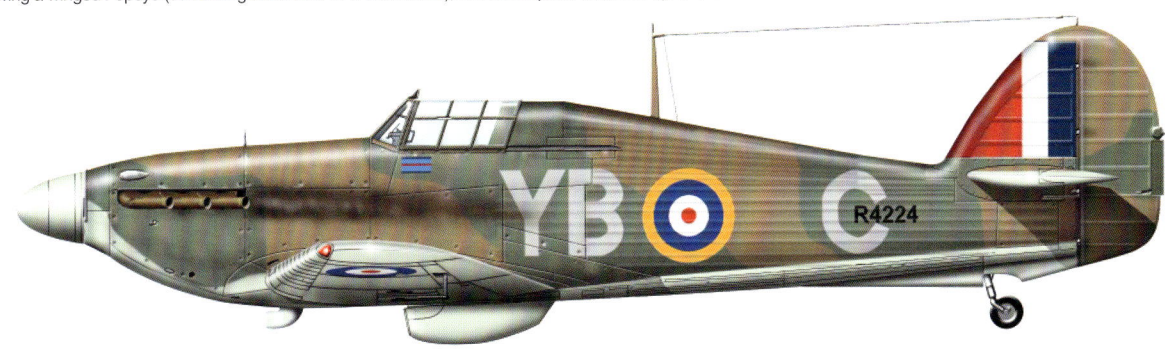

Hawker Hurricane Mk I (R4224) from No 17 Squadron, North Weald, England, September 1940. This plane's pilot, Squadron Leader A.G. Miller, took command of the unit after its former boss' death: Squadron Leader Cedric Williams was shot down in aerial combat on 18 August 1940. Given the task of defending British territory, No 17 Squadron was sent to the Far East in November 1941.

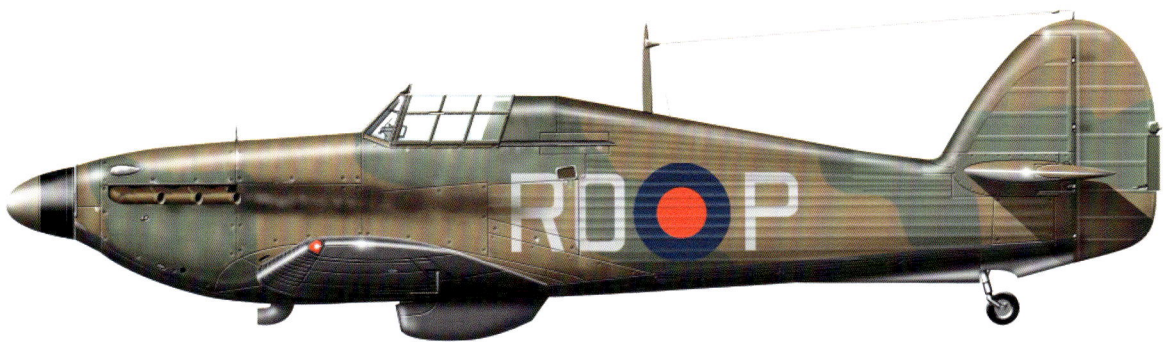

Hawker Hurricane Mk I (serial number unknown) from No 29 Squadron, Debden, England, September 1939. Shortly after the beginning of the war, this unit was re-equipped with Blenheim twin-engined fighters, particularly for night-time interception. This plane bears a Type B roundel (two colours) on the fuselage but none on the undersides.

Hawker Hurricane Mk I (P3522) from No 32 (the Royal) Squadron, Hawkinge, England, July 1940. This squadron received its Hurricanes a year before the beginning of the war and took part in the first phase of the Battle of Britain before being sent to the north of the British Isles until December 1940. The underside was painted sky blue and bore no roundels and this appeared at the beginning of June 1940. The 40" high letters were the biggest painted on a Hurricane.

Hawker Hurricane Mk I (serial number unknown) from No 43 (China-British) Squadron, Tangmere, England, July 1939. After taking part in the beginning of the Battle of Britain, No 43 Squadron was also sent to rest in the North of the British Isles where it carried out air defence and training missions.

Hawker Hurricane Mk I (serial number unknown) from No 46 (Uganda) Squadron, Bardufoss, Norway, mid-1940. This squadron was sent to Norway aboard the aircraft carrier HMS Glorious on 14 May 1940. At the end of the Norway expedition the surviving machines, though not properly equipped, returned to deck land on the aircraft carrier which itself was finally sunk on its way home to England, by the cruiser Scharnhorst; only two pilots survived the sinking… During this expedition, the Hurricanes had had their flanks and the underside of the fuselage and the tail fin painted sky grey.

Hawker Hurricane Mk I (P2764) from No 56 (Punjab) Squadron, North Weald, England, May 1940. After covering the Dunkirk evacuation (Operation Dynamo), this squadron fought during the whole of the Battle of Britain before becoming the first RAF Typhoon unit in November 1941. During the fighting in France, roundels were added under the wings in 15 May 1940, the one on the left being edged with yellow.

Hawker Hurricane Mk I (L1990) from No 56 (Punjab) Squadron, North Weald, England, 1939. This machine is wearing one of the camouflage schemes used in 1939 with a Type B roundel (two colours) obtained by modifying the original tricolour (A1) ones, large-sized medium sea grey fuselage markings, and black underside (left wing) and white (right wing), and aluminium (fuselage). L1990 was shot down by a Bf 109E near Portsmouth on 18 August 1940 and its pilot killed. At the time it was in No 601 Sqn.

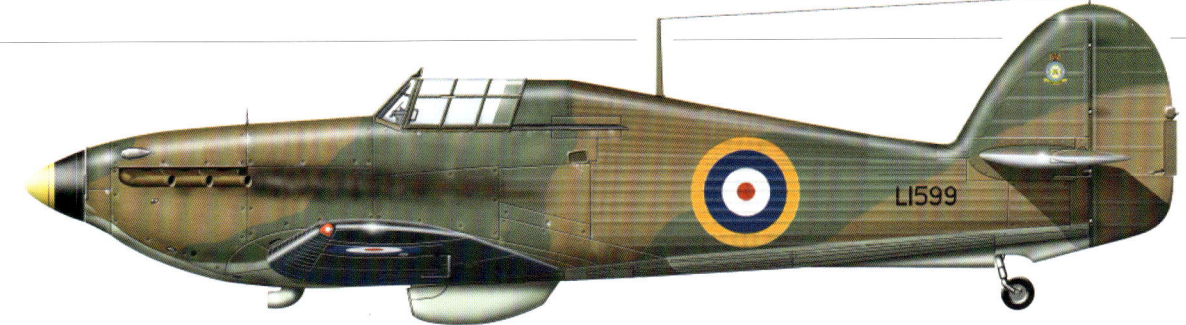

Hawker Hurricane Mk I (L1599) from No 56 (Punjab) Squadron, North Weald, England, May 1938. This plane, lost in a crash in Essex in April 1939, has been painted according to the regulations in effect in 1938 at the time the Hurricane entered service with the RAF, with in particular three colour (black, white and aluminium) undersides over which the serial number has been painted, a Type A1 roundel with a broad yellow border but no fuselage markings and no tail fin flash. The tail insignia was removed when the war started, the official texts stipulating that this could be done at any moment to make identifying the planes more difficult.

Hawker Hurricane Mk I (V7108) from No 71 (Eagle) Squadron, Kirton in Lindsey, England, 1941. No 71 was the first of the Eagle Squadrons, made up of American volunteers engaged in the RAF or RCAF. Formed in September 1940, it was at first given Brewster Buffalo Mk Is which it quickly exchanged for Hurricanes which it kept until August 1941. This plane bears the regulation camouflage for the period November 1940 to April 1941 with undersides sky blue and black left wing. The fuselage stripe, added later, partly covered the serial number.

Hawker Hurricane Mk I (P2575) from No 73 Squadron of the Advanced Air Striking Force, Rouvres, France, March 1940. Operating near the French Groups this unit's Hurricanes had a tricolour flag painted on the rudder like the French, with only the individual letter (medium sea grey) painted on the fuselage to avoid any possible confusion with Luftwaffe fighters.

Hawker Hurricane Mk I (V7524) from No 73 Squadron, El Adem, Egypt, February 1941. This squadron was at first used in the night fighter role during the Battle of Britain before being sent to Egypt in November 1940. This machines sports the regulation "desert" camouflage where sand (middle stone) replaced the traditional dark green; the undersides were painted sky blue which spread up the sides of the fuselage in the front to deceive the Italian AA guns during low-level attacks.

Hawker Hurricane Mk I (Z4189) from No 73 Squadron, Malta, 1942. On the right-hand emergency evacuation panel there is an insignia depicting a winged bomb. The underside has been painted sky blue.

Hawker Hurricane Mk I (L1833) from No 85 Squadron, Debden, England, September 1938. RAF fighters were hastily camouflaged during the Munich crisis in September 1938 and Type B roundels (two colours) on the fuselage were obtained by transforming the earlier ones. The underside could be painted in a variety of ways or left aluminium, but did not have any nationality markings.

Hawker Hurricane Mk I (serial number unknown) from No 85 Squadron, Lille Seclin, France, 6 December 1939 during King George VI's visit. The way in which the squadron insignia has been painted on the tail shows to which flight the plane belongs: at the tip for Flight B and on one of the sides for Flight A.

Hawker Hurricane Mk I (serial number unknown) from No 85 Squadron, Debden, England, June 1940. The tail fin flash and the roundel's yellow edge (whose width varied) were introduced by an official note dated 1 May 1940, especially for the units based or fighting in France.

Hawker Hurricane Mk I (P2923) from No 85 Squadron, Martlesham Heath, England, August 1940. After this squadron came back from France (with only four operational planes), where it had been part of the BEF's Air Component, it took part in the Battle of Britain. The underside has been covered with a substitute for the regulation sky – blue perhaps duck egg blue.

Hawker Hurricane Mk I (P3049) from No 85 Squadron, Kirton in Lindsey, England, beginning of 1940. This plane was occasionally used by two Free French pilots, Adjudants François de Labouchère and Emile Fayolle for night-time intruder operations which explains why it has been painted entirely Special Night (black). The squadron insignia, relocated under the windshield when the tail fin flash appeared, has been retained.

Hawker Hurricane Mk I (P2544) from No 80 Squadron, Amriyah, Palestine, December 1940. After starting the war with Gloster Gladiators, this squadron took part in the Greek Campaign before being sent to the Middle East (Syria with detachments in Palestine and Cyprus). Note the unusual size of the fin flash whose colours are the same width.

Hawker Hurricane Mk I (serial number unknown) from No 87 (United Provinces) Squadron, Lille, France, March 1940. The snake, usually painted within the tail insignia was removed in December 1939. This plane was from the beginning of the production series (fabric-covered wings and Watts two-bladed propeller) and had its fuselage underside painted aluminium with black and white wings.

Hawker Hurricane Mk I (L1774) from No 87 (United Provinces) Squadron, Lille, France, May 1940. After being part of the BEF's Air Component, this squadron took part in the whole of the Battle of Britain and was given Mark IIs at the end of 1940. The yellow-edged roundel and the fin flash were introduced with an official note on 1 May 1940.

Hawker Hurricane Mk I (P2798) from No 87 (United Provinces) Squadron, Scilly Isles, England, May 1941. Pilot: Squadron Leader Ian "Widge" Gleed. Based in the Scilly Isles in the Spring of 1941, this plane was used for night time intruder operations in its original livery and especially the insignia showing a cat smashing a swastika and was totally painted Special Night black. P/O Ivor Badger shot down an Arado Ar 196 on 19 May 1941 with this plane.

Hawker Hurricane Mk I (L1581) from No 111 Squadron, Villacoublay, France, July 1938. A detachment from this squadron took part in the flypast over Paris for the 14 July 1938 celebrations, the planes being indeed based temporarily in the Paris suburbs. The colour the squadron number has been painted indicates the Flight the plane belonged to: blue, yellow and red.

Hawker Hurricane Mk I (serial number unknown) from No 111 Squadron, Wick, Scotland, winter 1939-1940. The Type A roundel was introduced on the fuselage in an official note dated 21 November 1939. On this machine the squadron code (JU) has been placed in front of the roundel on both sides of he fuselage.

Hawker Hurricane Mk I (V6701) from No 111 Squadron, Dyce, England, February 1941. Given the task of protecting the Dunkirk evacuation, this squadron took part in the first part of the Battle of Britain then was sent to Scotland to rest from September 1940 to July 1941. The sky blue fuselage stripe has partly covered the serial number and the undersides, according to the regulations of the period are sky coloured except the left wing which was black.

Hawker Hurricane Mk I (xx939) from No 123 (East India) Squadron, Abadan, Persia, November 1942. This unit received Hurricanes to replace its Gladiators in November 1941 and used them for the air defence of Persia (present-day Iran) until May 1943. The first two figures of this plane's serial number, whose underside is either azure blue or light Mediterranean blue, have been covered by a coat of fresh dark earth.

Hawker Hurricane Mk I (serial number unknown) from No 145 Squadron, Croydon, England, June 1940. This machine's underside has been painted with a substitute for the regulation grey green which explains why there are no roundels under the wings and way the fuselage colour have been delimited lower down. After beginning the war on Blenheims, No145 Sqn replaced them with Hurricanes in March 1940 and then was equipped with Spitfires in January 1941.

Hawker Hurricane Mk I (serial number unknown) from No 151 Squadron, Sealand, England, July 1939. This machine whose serial number has been deliberately masked, bears the regulation camouflage for the beginning of the war, with the two-coloured under surfaces (black on the left and white) without any roundels; only the planes based in France had these. The fuselage roundel has been obtained by transforming the regulation model, the outer yellow and central white sections having been removed.

Hawker Hurricane Mk I (L1754) from No 151 Squadron, Martlesham Heath, England, May-June 1940. This squadron took part in the fighting in France whilst remaining in England. Progressively specialising in the night-fighter role, it was given Boulton Paul Defiants in November 1940. Apart from its fin flash – wider at the front, this plane differs by having its fuselage roundel base covered with Special Night (black).

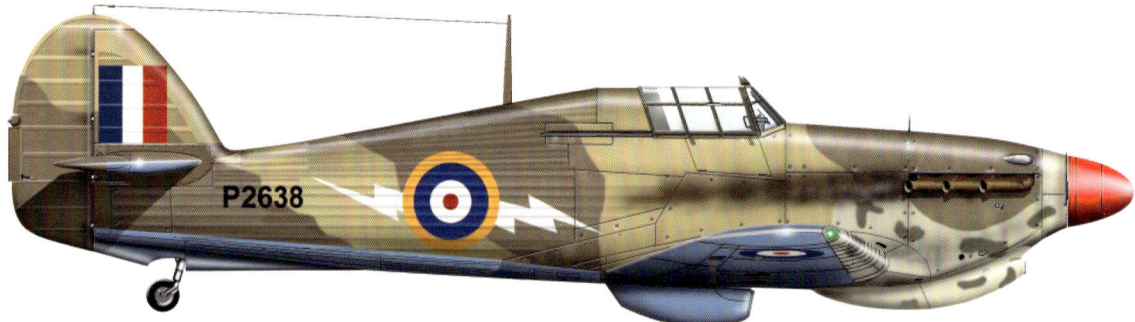

Hawker Hurricane Mk I (P2638) from No 208 Squadron, Heliopolis, Egypt, July 1942. Originally equipped with Lysanders, one of this squadron's flights was equipped with Hurricanes in November 1940. The special camouflage on the front of this machine, nicknamed "sand and spinach", inspired by the Italian camouflage schemes was intended to trick enemy AA gunners during low level attacks.

Hawker Hurricane Mk I (W9291) from No 213 (Ceylon) Squadron, Ismailia, Egypt, November 1941. Having received some Hurricanes in January 1939, this squadron was sent to Egypt in June 1941 and then detached to Syria and Cyprus. Used mainly for nighttime missions, this plane has been entirely painted with Special Night (black) and all its markings, roundels and individual letter, have been considerably reduced.

Hawker Hurricane Mk I (V7203) from No 242 (Canadian) Squadron, Collishall, England, July 1940. The pilot of this plane, Sub-Lieutenant Richard Exton Gardner, RN, was normally in the Royal Navy but was assigned to the RAF at the time of the Battle of Britain. After scoring his first kill on 10 July, "Jimmy" Gardner obtained "ace" status the following September and then distinguished himself in the Mediterranean flying a Fairey Fulmar, on his return to the Navy. This plane bears the unit's insignia, a caricature of Hitler being kicked up the behind…

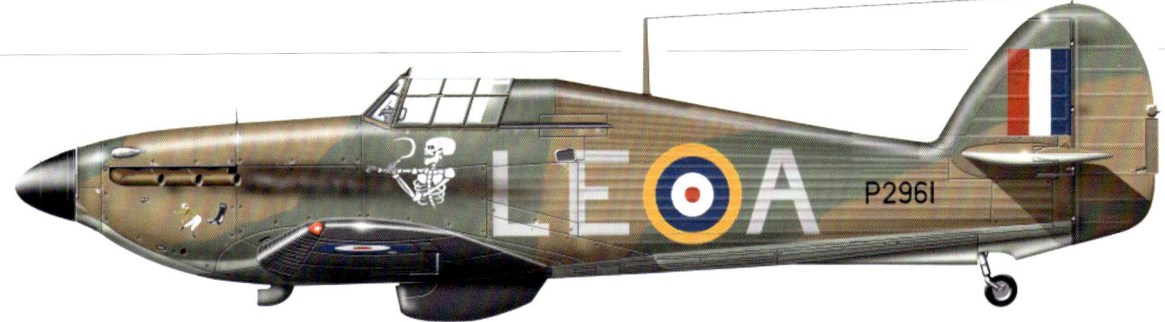

Hawker Hurricane Mk I (P2961) from No 242 (Canadian) Squadron, January 1941. Pilot: flight Officer William Lidstone "Willie" McKnight. This Canadian, awarded the DFC, was killed in an accident after the Battle of Britain, on 12 January 1941. At the time he had scored 16.5 confirmed kills including a hat trick on 30 August 1940.

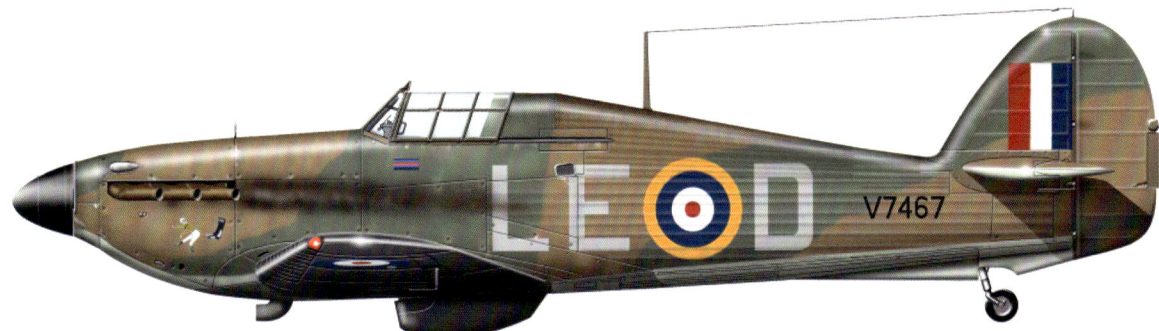

Hawker Hurricane Mk I (V7467) from No 242 Squadron, January 1942. This was the machine of the famous "legless pilot", Squadron Leader Douglas Robert Stewart Bader, who had an accident in 1931 and continued to fly with artificial legs. Engaged in the RAF, Bader became the CO of No 242 Squadron, a unit made up mainly of Canadians, and was shot down in aerial combat on 9 August 1941. A POW until the end of the war, especially in Colditz, he had scored 22 kills before being captured which makes him one of the greatest Hurricane aces.

Hawker Hurricane Mk I (V6846) from No 247 (China-British) Squadron. Aboard this plane built by Gloster, Sous-Lieutenant Claude Hellès of the FAFL (Free French) scored one kill – a Junkers Ju 88 – on 22 July 1941. Note the small sized roundels and yellow edge, and the way in which the markings, also smaller and dull red in colour, have been painted behind it.

Hawker Hurricane Mk I (V6873) from No 257 (Burma) Squadron, North Weald, England, December 1940. Pilot: Squadron Leader Roland Robert Stanford Tuck. Tuck started the war in May 1940 on Spitfires in No 92 Sqn before being promoted to Squadron Leader of No 257 Sqn, equipped with Hurricanes. Shot down in February 1942 and a POW until the end of the conflict, he had scored 27 kills.

Hawker Hurricane Mk I (serial number unknown) from No 257 (Burma) Squadron, Colishall, England, March 1941. Because some photographs of this squadron's planes had been published in the newspapers, its fuselage markings were changed from "DT" to "FM" in May 1940. One of the particularities of No257 Sqn was that in June 1940, it exchanged its Spitfires for Hurricanes which it used for the whole of the Battle of Britain and until July 1942 when it converted to Typhoons.

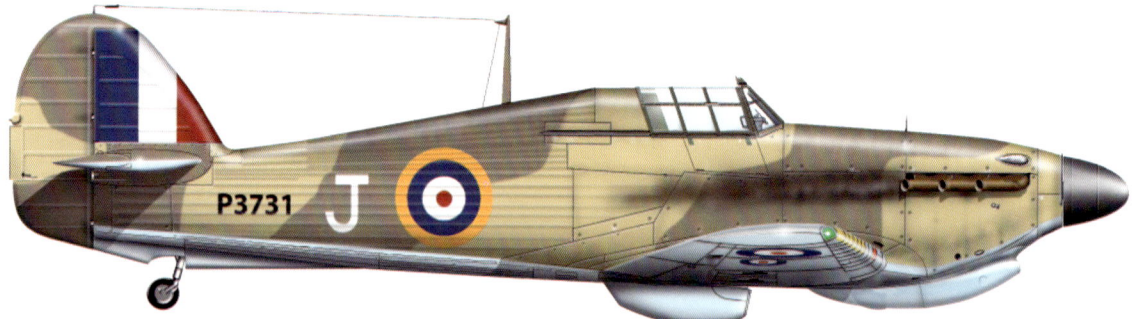

Hawker Hurricane Mk I (P3731) from No 261 Squadron, Ta' Qali, Malta, June 1941. With standard desert camouflage but sky blue lower surfaces, this plane was part of the contingent launched from the aircraft carrier HMS Argus to reinforce Malta's defences. It was used by several aces in this theatre and in particular by Sergeant Fred Robertson. No 261 Sqn was formed in August 1940 from the Malta Defence Flight and comprised a mixed strength of Gladiator biplanes and Hurricanes.

Hawker Hurricane Mk I (P3128) from No 303 (Warsaw-Kosciusko) Squadron, Northolt, England, August 1940. Created in August 1940 with personnel and pilots who had fled Poland, this squadron took part in the first phase of the Battle of Britain before being sent to the North to rest. The insignia of the 111. Eskadara "Warsaw-Kosciusko" was painted either behind the canopy as here or below the windshield, whilst the blue stripe most likely indicates that this was the Flight Commander's plane.

Hawker Hurricane Mk I (V7741) from No 306 (City of Torun) Squadron, Church Stanton, England, February 1941. Formed in August 1940, this squadron received its Hurricane Mark IIAs when it settled on the base at Northolt in April 1941. The insignia painted under the exhaust pipes on both sides is the squadron's, whereas a small Polish checkerboard was added to the rear inside the fuselage markings, a very common practice in this unit.

Hawker Hurricane Mk I (P3145) from No 310 (Czechoslovak) Squadron, Duxford, England, September 1940. This squadron, made up of Czech pilots who had fled their country after the German invasion, was formed in July 1940 and used Hurricane Mk Is until March 1941. This machine's code is not regulation because the letters are white (or light grey) and not medium sea grey.

Hawker Hurricane Mk I (L1926) from No 312 (Czechoslovak) Squadron, Speke, England, October 1940. Pilot: Pilot Officer Alois Vasalko. This Czech fought in France with GCI/5, the French Air Force's highest scoring unit before he joined No 312 Sqn formed in August 1940. After scoring one kill during the Battle of Britain, Vasalko was appointed commander of a Wing at Exeter but died a few weeks later when he collided in flight with an Fw 190 on 23 June 1942. As for the "L1926" it was transferred to No 55 OTU and destroyed on landing on 15 April 1941.

Hawker Hurricane Mk I (P2827) from No 315 (Deblin) Squadron, Speke, England, June 1941. Formed in February 1941 with Polish pilots, this squadron only used its Hurricanes for a few weeks since it was given Spitfires in July the same year. According to the unit regulations, the national checkerboard was painted in front of the windshield on both sides of the fuselage.

Hawker Hurricane Mk I (serial number unknown) from No 501 (City of Bristol/County of Gloucester) Squadron, Kenley, England, December 1940. Pilot: P/O Kenneth McKenzie. Equipped with Hurricanes from March 1939, this unit was given the task of defending the AASF in France from its English base before taking part in the whole of the Battle of Britain.

Hawker Hurricane Mk I (L1659) from No 501 (City of Bristol/ County of Gloucester) Squadron, Tangmere, England, March 1940. This plane bears the camouflage scheme introduced in November 1939 with fuselage roundels without yellow borders, with larger codes overlapping the serial number.

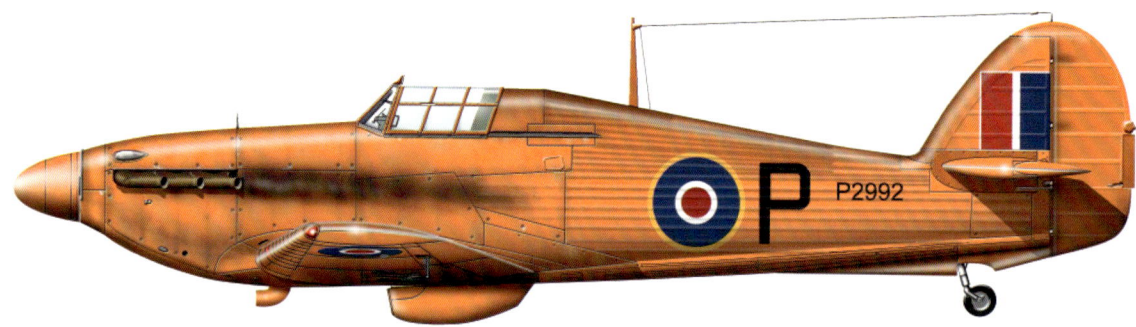

Hawker Hurricane Mk I (P2992) from No 257 Squadron, Castle Camps, England, 1943. Formed in June 1943, this squadron was given the task of calibrating radar and developing localisation and instrument landing systems. For this, the various types it used (Blenheims, Hornet Moths, Spitfires etc.) were painted bright colours like this orange-red Hurricane.

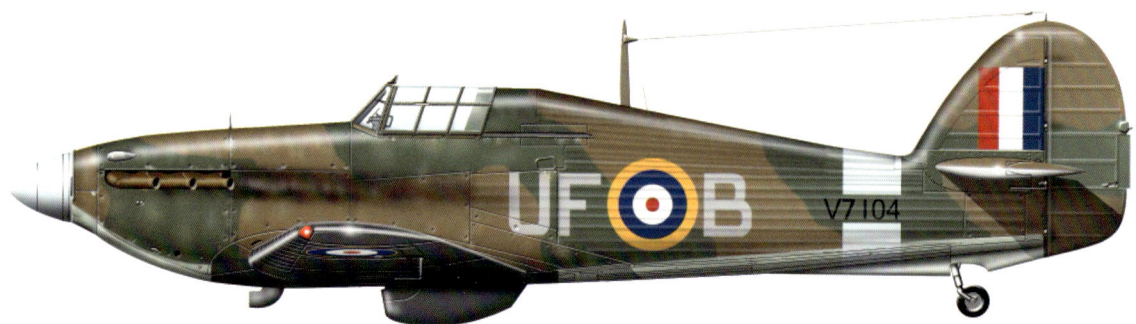

Hawker Hurricane Mk I (V7104) from No 601 (County of London) Squadron, Northolt, England, beginning of 1941. Becoming a fighter squadron when it received its Hurricanes, in August of the following year No601 became one of the rare units equipped with the Bell Airacobra I. The underside of the left wing has been painted black, a feature which was reintroduced in November 1940 whilst the sky blue fuselage stripe was broken by the serial number.

Hawker Hurricane Mk I (serial number unknown) from No 615 (County of Surrey) Squadron, Northolt, England, August 1940. After taking part in the Battle of Britain, this squadron which had been converted to Hurricanes just before the French Campaign, was sent to the Far East (India and Burma).

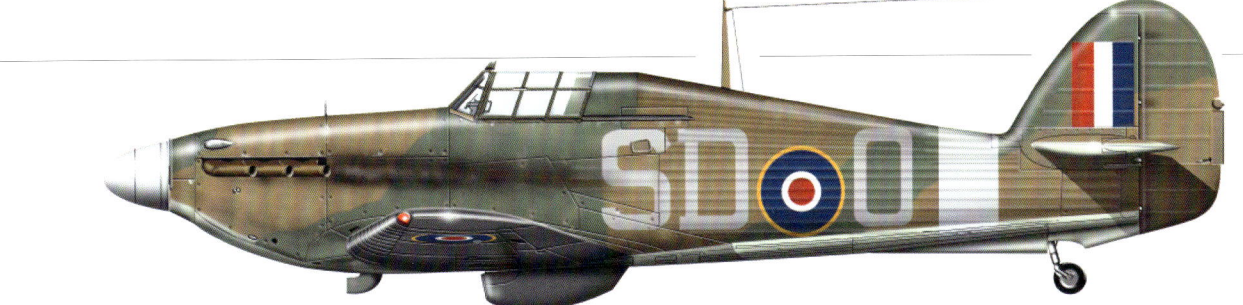

Hawker Hurricane Mk I (serial number unknown) from No 615 (County of Surrey) Squadron, Northolt, England, end of 1940. This plane's pilot, Adjudant René Mouchotte, reached England in 1940 and became the first foreigner to be promoted to Flight Commander in the RAF and the first Frenchman to lead an RAF fighter squadron. After taking part in the creation of No 340 (Ile-de-France) and No 341 (Alsace), Squadrons, Mouchotte was shot down on 27 August 1943.

Hawker Hurricane Mk I (Z2703) from No 615 Squadron, Kenley, England, May 1941. This plane is a subscription aircraft, put up by the inhabitants of Croydon, the town near the Kenley base, and presented to the RAF; the town's arms have been painted under the canopy just above the first letter of the code.

Hawker Hurricane Mk I (Z4932) from the Royal Navy Fighter Squadron, Maddalena, Libya, December 1941. "Kiwi" was a Hurricane used frequently by Sub-Lieutenant M. Fell at the end of 1941 and was sot down near Martuba on 15 January the following year. The RNFS had been created by amalgamating Nos 803, 805 and 806 NAS in No 269 Wing based in Egypt and was equipped with Martlets (the English name for the Grumann Wildcat) and strictly standard Hurricanes without any naval equipment.

Hawker Hurricane Mk I (L2006) from 11 Group Pilot Pool, Sutton Bridge, England, 1939. This unit was given the task of training pilots and for this was equipped with Hurricanes, Gladiators, Harvards, Masters and even Battles; it became No 6 OTU (Operational Training Unit) in March 1940. This Hurricane whose underside was painted yellow like all British training aircraft was, as the story goes, the plane which had the most accidents at Sutton Bridge base.

Hawker Hurricane Mk I (Z4936) from the Merchant Ship Fighter Unit (MSFU), Speke, England, 1942. This unit was given the job of training the Hurricane pilots aboard catapult-equipped merchantmen for convoy protection. This plane's camouflage was the Temperate Sea Scheme comprising dark sea grey and dark slate grey on the upper surfaces and sky grey undersides, which was also used for the code letters.

Hawker Hurricane Mk I (Z4667) from the Merchant Ship Fighter Unit, Speke, England. The planes to be catapulted from a CAM, and therefore "disposable", were at first merely Hurricanes struck off by Fighter Command, equipped with catapult rings and re-named "Sea Hurricane Mk IA". The MFSU used several fuselage codes corresponding most likely to the units it had based in Canada, USSR or Gibraltar.

Hawker Hurricane Mk I (Z4040) from No 71 Operational Conversion Unit (OCU), Ismailia, Egypt, 1943. The essential task of this unit was to train pilots for flying in desert conditions, but it also took part in defensive operations particularly over the Suez Canal Zone.

Hawker Hurricane Mk I (P3039) from No 55 OTU, Aston Down, England, 1942. Given the job of training Fighter Command pilots, this unit was equipped with various types of machines (Hurricanes, Blenheims, Masters and Defiants) bearing several fuselage codes (UW, EH, PA, ZX, etc.).

Hawker Hurricane Mk I (V7173) from No 59 OTU, Turnhouse, England, 1943. This unit, given the task of training single seat fighter pilots, was given Typhoons in addition to its complement of Hurricanes in August 1943 and was disbanded the following year. The unpainted canopy frame shows that this has most likely just been replaced.

Hawker Hurricane Mk I (Z4791) from the Empire Central Flying School, Hullavington, England, September 1942. The ECFS was made up of several squadrons and flights, for training future RAF instructors and putting new equipment into service.

Hawker Hurricane Mk I (L4573) from No 2 Squadron, Indian Air Force, Risalpur, India, December 1942. Created in April 1941 and at first equipped with Westland Wapitis and Lysanders, this squadron received its Hurricanes in September 1942 with which it took part in the Burma Campaign.

Hawker Hurricane Mk I (XX289) from No 3 (SAAF) Squadron, Abyssinia, mid-1940. Created in 1940, this squadron fought in East Africa and in North Africa before taking part in the Italian Campaign. As with all SAAF planes at the time, the red in the national colours were replaced with orange.

HURRICANE MARK II

DURING THE FIGHTING IN FRANCE, the first trials of a new version of the Hurricane, called logically the Mark II, were carried out in Great Britain. It was indeed on 11 June 1940 that Philip Lucas took P3269 up from Langley aerodrome on its maiden flight. This was a machine equipped with the new Merlin XX engine using 100 octane fuel instead of the previous 87. This powerplant also had a two-speed supercharger ("FS" for Full Supercharge ratio from 18 040 ft (5 500 m) and "MS" for Moderate Supercharge, more economical below that rpm level) which was adjustable by the pilot depending on external air pressure, ensuring the best performance both at high and medium altitudes.

Fitting this new powerplant had been decided upon because it enabled a more effective version of the fighter (rated first at 1 185 bhp then 1 280 bhp on take-off) to be put into service immediately without disturbing the production lines since the rest of the machine was almost unchanged. The Merlin XX was also slightly longer than previous engines so the fuselage was therefore lengthened accordingly by adding a 4 ½ in (11-cm) section in front of the cockpit which also improved the aircraft's stability by moving the centre of gravity slightly forwards. The carburettor air intake on the underside in front of the wheel wells was also modified and placed 3 in (7.5 cm) further back, and the radiator was enlarged.

Apart from better performances, the new engine was also more reliable since it was now cooled using a 30% glycol (a highly inflammable liquid) and 70% water mixture, thus reducing the risks of fire; but it was also more effective since its operating temperature was reduced by 70°, ensuring a longer life and increased reliability.

The first variant – the Mark IIA

As the trials had turned out to be conclusive, with the aircraft reaching speeds of 350 mph at 10 825 ft (560 kph at 3 300 m)[1], series production was launched in the middle of August 1940, thirty or so examples being delivered by the middle of September. Originally it was intended for the Hurricane Mk II to be armed with twelve 7.7 mm Browning machine guns but there were just not enough of these weapons available at this critical time for the RAF, meaning that they were reduced to eight like on the previous version.

Once again No 111 Squadron was the first unit to be equipped with the Hurricane Mk IIA in September 1940. Although 12.5 mph (20 kph) slower than a Spitfire, the Mk IIA was the fastest of all the Hurricanes and was the only one of this version to take part in the final phases of the Battle of Britain.

Already fighting in North Africa and Europe, the Hurricane was also sent to a new, more distant front, to replace less useful machines. Indeed

Above.
« The Last of the many » (PZ865, le dernier de beaucoup) est un Mark IIC, The "Last of the Many" (PZ865) was a Mark IIC, the last of the 14 533 Hurricanes built. It was never delivered to an operational unit and took part in various competition demonstrations after the war and is nowadays preserved, in flying condition, with the Battle of Britain Memorial Flight.

---

1. *Slower than the Spitfire, the Mk II was however the fastest of the Hurricanes.*

Opposite.
Hurricane Mk II from the beginning of the production series, recognisable because of the little mast on the rudder. (NASA)

Above.
A flight of Hurricane Mk IIDs (Trop) from No 6 Squadron taking off in the desert. Because they were so effective, especially against the Afrika Korps armour, the unit's machines earned the nickname of "Flying Can Openers". (IWM)

during the days following Pearl Harbour and the Japanese advances in Far-East Asia, fifty or so Mk IIs were shipped in their crates to Singapore with 24 pilots in order to form the basis of five squadrons. When they arrived on 3 January 1942, the planes were assembled and made operational in less than two days; the pilots made up No 232 Squadron which was declared operational on the 18 January and amalgamated with No 488 Squadron RNZAF equipped with Buffaloes. They were immediately thrown into the battle and the first clashes, mainly with Japanese Ki-43s, were not long in coming, with the unit scoring its first kills and thus its first losses as of 20 January. By the end of the same month, a new contingent of 48 Hurricanes Mk IIAs were taken by aircraft carrier to Sumatra where thirty or so of them were destroyed on the ground during a Japanese air raid on 7 February. After Singapore fell, the survivors of No 232 Squadron were in turn transferred to Sumatra which they had to leave quickly after heavy fighting in order to escape to Java. At that moment only 18 operational fighters were left, a figure which fell to two by the following 7 March. After the invasion of Java the surviving Hurricanes were destroyed on the spot and all the pilots evacuated to Australia by boat together with the only unassembled Hurricane which thereby became the only one of this type to be used, for training purposes, by the RAAF.

The Mark IIB

At the beginning of 1940, the authorities asked Hawkers to see whether the armament on the Hurricane could be reinforced, increasing it to twelve machine guns with 6 000 rounds, its original configuration.

As this modification risked disrupting the production rate during one of Great Britain's most critical periods, it was only authorised in November 1940 when the manufacturer presented a new wing specially designed to take not only extra weapons but also bomb launchers, with all the necessary cabling.

This variant was at first called the Mk IIA Series 2 then finally Mk IIB from April 1941 onwards; it differed in having a slightly longer propeller spinner, a tail wheel (now fitted with a shock absorber) sunk well ino the slightly modified rear keel and especially its armament, increased to twelve 7.7 mm Browning machine guns in the wings, the two extra pairs of guns being fitted into the wing leading edge outside the original four weapons.

Moreover, two strong points were added under the wings for carrying (two 250-lb or 500-lb) bombs, or 44-gallon drop tanks or 90-gall fixed tanks for convoying which almost doubled the amount of fuel carried.

The first examples came off the Hawker and Gloster production lines in October 1940 and final production amounted to 3 100 examples to which a few others must be added, obtained by modifying Hurricane Mk Is.

With their dozen machine guns (some only had ten to reduce take off weight slightly and not to over-penalise the aircraft's performances), the Mk IIB rapidly nicknamed the "Hurribomber" started to operate on the continent, especially over enemy-occupied France on low altitude day and night intruder missions. The first squadron equipped with the new variant was No 56 at Duxford, with No 607 starting to use them at the very end of October 1941 especially on ground attack missions over the continent.

The RAF no longer used the Hurricane as a day fighter on the Western Front after the disastrous landing at Dieppe (in August 1942). It was less effective than the German fighters (the Bf 109F and especially the Fw 190A) in this role, even with its Merlin XX, so it had to hand over to the Spitfire and get used to the new role in which it was to excel until the end of the war, especially in the Far East, that of ground attack.

Hurricane Mk IIB Trop

The Hawker Hurricane Mk IIBs sent to North Africa were "tropicalised", in the field to begin with, their engines fitted with a Voke or Rolls Royce dust filter in a fairing located under the nose in front of the carburettor air intake. This "aesthetic" modification was on top of a desert survival kit comprising in particular a water container located behind the cockpit. In 1939 the first "tropicalisation" trials were carried out on a few, specially modified Mk Is and sent to Khartoum.

The Mark IIC

This variant goes back to an official request dating from 1935 for a fighter armed with four 20-mm cannon. Hawker's had originally intended to equip its Hurricane like this but they thought the configuration penalised the plane's performance too much for a single-seat, single-engined fighter. In 1939, two 30-mm Oerlikon cannon had been installed under the wings of a Hurricane Mk I, Serial Number L1750, and the results of the tests had encouraged Sydney Camm to carry on in this direction as soon as possible.

While the Battle of Britain was raging, one fighter (Serial Number V7360) whose wings had been damaged, was fitted with new ones at the Langley

Below.
Two Hurricane Mk IIC Night Intruders, painted totally black (Special Night) and with special markings adapted to their nighttime missions. Note the metal exhaust dampeners in front of the cockpit, hiding the exhaust from the pilot's sight.

Above.
Hurricane Mk (Met) IIC from No 521 Squadron, specialising in weather reconnaissance. For this special role, this machine was unarmed; the only things left were parts of the wing cannon barrel sleeves.

Above.
Hurricane Mk IICs from No 3 Squadron in flight. This unit was sent to Scotland after the French Campaign and given the job of protecting the naval base at Scapa Flow. After receiving Mk IICs, it used them for intruder operations before replacing them in February 1943 with Hawker Typhoons.

factory, armed with four belt-fed Hispano cannon and equipped with a heating system. This aircraft took to the air for the first time on 5 December 1940. Subsequently several other examples were modified in the same way and tried out at the A & AEE, reaching 337.5 mph at 16 400 ft (540 kph at 5 000m) with a loaded weight of 7 876 lb (3 580 kg). Trials were also carried out with fighters fitted with Voke filters; their performance dropped quite considerably (321 mph / 515 kph top speed).

As priority had been given to cannon production for the Bristol Beaufighter during the Blitz in 1940-1941, it was only during the spring of 1941 that the new version officially made its appearance. This was in fact a Hurricane Mk IIA equipped with a slightly longer propeller spinner, armed with four 20-mm Hispano Mk II cannon in the wings in place of the machine guns, and given the designation Hurricane Mk IIC in June 1941.

Like its predecessor, the Mk IIB, it could also carry two 250-lb or two 500-lb bombs, or drop tanks. The first two units to receive the Mk IIC were No 3 and No 257 Squadrons, the latter commanded at the time by the ace Stanford Tuck who had distinguished himself during the Battle of Britain.

Originally intended for daytime attack operations over the continent, the Mk IIC was used in this role until 1943 when it was replaced by another of the Hawker stable's thoroughbreds, the Typhoon. Its role was then changed and it served essentially at night for "intruder" or interceptor missions.

One of the more original tactics used by the Hurricane Mk IICs based in England consisted in intercepting German bombers in the neighbourhood of their bases when they were returning from their missions, the pilots and planes already worn out by the mission being easy preys for these well-armed adversaries. One of the more talented of these "intruders" was the Czech K.M. Kuttlewascher, from No1 Squadron who managed to shoot down three Heinkel 111s in a single night-time mission on 2 May 1942, and whose tally reached finally reached eighteen confirmed kills.

A small series of planes specially equipped for the night fighter role and sometimes called NF Mk IICs was made at the end of 1941. They were distinguished by an AI Mk IV radar housed in a container looking like a 44-gallon drop tank fitted to the wing (another tank, a real one, was fitted to the other wing, in order to balance the plane). A dozen of these machines was delivered to No 245 Squadron at Middle Wallop at the beginning of 1942 and used until the autumn of the same year.

At the height of its career, during the winter of 1941-1942, thirty Fighter Command squadrons based in Great Britain were quipped with Hurricane Mk IICs to which must be added ten others operating in the Middle East.

SPECIFICATIONS HURRICANE MARK IIC

Type: Single seat fighter
Powerplant: One V-12 liquid-cooled Rolls Royce Merlin XX rated at 1 185 bhp at 20990 ft (6 400m)
Dimensions
Length: 32 ft 3 in (9,84 m)
Height: 13 ft 1 in (3,99 m)
Wingspan: 40 ft (12,19 m)
Wing Surface: 257.990 sq ft (23,97 m²)
Weight (empty): 4 569 lb (2 118 kg)

Weight (fully laden): 6 586 lb (2 994 kg)
Performances
Maximum speed: 341 mph (547 km/h) at 20 990 ft (6 400m)
Maximum range: 603 miles (965 km)
Operational Ceiling 35 980 ft (10 970 m)
Armament
Four 20-mm (0.79 in) wing-mounted Hispano cannon and two 250 or 500-lb (110 or 230 kg) bombs.

Above.
A group of Hurricane Mk IIDs from No 6 Squadron in flight. No 6 Squadron was the main user of this anti-tank version in North Africa. The planes sport complete fuselage codes with non-regulation colour variations for the individual letters. (IWM)

Opposite.
Hurricane Mk X from the Fighter Leaders School at Millfield in 1944. The Canadian-made Hurricanes were outwardly identical to the British-made ones.

In the summer of 1943, this variant was still in service in twenty-one squadrons fighting in the Far East (India and Burma, etc.) so much so that in the end there were no less than eighty squadrons equipped with Mk IICs. Production of this variant only ceased in September 1944, but it is not known how many examples were actually made (4 711 according to a lot of sources) as there is no existing account and a lot of damaged planes were brought up to IIC standard after being repaired.

The Desert Air Force also used the Hurricane in great numbers but because of the appearance of more effective versions of the Messerschmitt Bf 109 (the E-7 and especially the F), its role as an interceptor was gradually changed to that of ground attack from June 1941 onwards, the "Hurribombers" distinguishing themselves in particular during the Battle of El Alamein in October 1942. On this occasion they carried out more than 800 sorties, the six Hurricane squadrons used destroying forty or so tanks and more than 400 miscellaneous vehicles – armoured or otherwise – for eleven pilots shot down.

The Mark IID

This variant, the last of the Mk IIs, was in reality a Hurricane Mk IIB armed with two 40-mm anti-tank cannon[2] carried in underwing gondolas; the Browning machine guns loaded with tracer bullets had been retained enabling the pilot to correct his aim. The Mk IID was designed specially for destroying tanks and other armoured vehicles, which were not affected by small calibre fire and which were therefore very difficult to hit with normal bombing.

The first Mk IID flew on 18 September 1941 and deliveries started at the start of the following year. The wings had been reinforced in order to take the extra load, the machine being able to withstand 4G with an all up weight of 8 540 lb (3 881 kg).

From the 93rd example onwards, apart from the armament, pilot protection was also improved, armour being added to the engine and radiator, increasing the new version's total weight and reducing its performances.

---

2. At first, Rolls Royce BFs (Belt-fed) with 12 rounds each were fitted, but replaced very quickly by 15-round Vickers Ss with which were more reliable and more effective.

Opposite.
One of No 151 Wing's Mk IIs based at Vaenga (on the Kola Isthmus) which were used to get Soviet pilots used to the Hurricane. After a few weeks on the spot, the machines were handed over to the Soviet Air Force. (IWM)

A group of Hurricane Mk IICs (Trop) from No 94 Squadron in flight. This Desert Air Force Squadron, as indicated by the spinners painted red, was for a time partially equipped with Kittyhawk and finally abandoned its Hurricane in favor of Spitfire in April 1944. (IWM)

The prototype of this new version, in fact a modified Mk IIA, flew for the first time on 18 September 1941 and about 300 machines were produced.

Only two RAF squadrons based in Great Britain used the Mk IID, No 184 and No 164, based at Colerne[3], all the other examples being dispatched overseas, in particular to the Middle East where No 6 Squadron initially based in Egypt, used its "Flying Can Openers" successfully supporting Free French Forces surrounded by the Afrika Korps at Bir Hakeim in May-June 1942. A year later twenty squadrons were still equipped with Hurricanes, five of them converting to Spitfires, but the others continuing the fight in Sicily, Italy and then in the Balkans. Stable, well-protected, formidably armed despite a reduced top speed due to the increased weight, the Hurricane Mk IID was considered to be the best anti-tank aircraft used by the RAF during WWII, even better than the Typhoon, which was given much more "publicity".

The Mk IID was also used successfully in the Far East (India, Burma and Ceylon) alongside the previous variants (Mk IIB and C). The first examples of the Hurricane reached Burma in January 1942 when thirty Mk IIAs originally intended for Singapore were re-routed to Rangoon. Rapidly joined by two other squadrons also intended for Singapore, these machines fought under very difficult conditions, from makeshift strips in the jungle, so much so that by the following March, only six machines were still operational. After fierce fighting, the units fell back on Jessore, in Bengal where they were given two variants (MK IIB and IIC) better adapted to their ground attack role. After the Japanese occupied Burma, new reinforcements were sent to India and in June 1942 there were eleven Hurricane squadrons[4] stationed there, a number that increased to sixteen when Burma was re-conquered the following year, 150 Mk IIDs having been brought in to reinforce them. From mid-1944, most of the Hurricane squadrons operating in the Far East had converted to Thunderbolts, with only two using the Mark IV (see next chapter) almost until the end of the war.

Hurricanes Mark X, XI and XII

Well aware that the factories in Great Britain would not be able to satisfy demand, the RAF's needs as well as potential foreign Hurricane customers, Hawker very early on envisaged "delocalising" part of its production to Canada. Twenty fighters were therefore sent there in October 1938 in order to be used as "models" for setting set up production lines.

The Canadian Car and Foundry C° based at Fort William, Ontario, started producing Mk Is under licence originally intended to equip a single RCAF fighter squadron, No 1, a unit which was sent to Great Britain in May 1940. The first time a Canadian Hurricane flew was in January 1940 and this version was then followed by a first batch of 340 machines called Mark X, powered by a Packard Merlin 28 (identical to the Rolls Royce XX) rated at 1 300 bhp and armed with eight .303 machine guns. These planes were mainly equipped like English machines and were followed by a second batch of 126 Mark Xs produced during the first six months of 1942, and equipped with Canadian equipment; most of them were kept in Canada and used for training.

This variant was followed by 150 Mark XIs, overall identical to the previous variants (same Packard 28) but with special equipment for the RCAF. Most of these planes were sent to Great Britain whereas some examples were delivered to the USSR or converted to Hurricane Mk XIB standard and armed with twelve machine guns.

The main Canadian-built version was the Mark XII, in fact a Mk IIB powered by a Packard Merlin 29 rated at 1 300 bhp and armed either with twelve machine guns (Mk XIIA) or four 20-mm cannon (Mk XIIB or Mk XIIC, identical to the Mk IIB and Mk IIC). Here again, certain Mk XIIAs were converted into Sea Hurricane Mk XIIAs.

In all 1 451 examples of the Hurricane were made in Canada under licence until the summer of 1943, representing 10% of total production of the machine.

---

3. Most likely with the machines from the beginning of the production series that had less armour.
4. Nos 17 and 615 at Jessore (Bengal), Nos 30 and 261 at Colombo (Ceylan), Nos 67, 79, 136 and 146 at Alipore (India), No 258 at Trincomalee, No 681 (a recce unit) at Pandaveswar and No 135 at Calcutta. During the Battle of Imphal (March-July 1944), Hurricanes were still serving in Nos 5, 11, 28, 34, 42 and 113 Squadrons, as well as in No 1 Squadron, Indian Air Force.

Hawker Hurricane Mk IIC (BE581) from No 1 Squadron, Redhill, England, April 1942. No 1 received its Mark IIs in January 1942 and used them for sweeps or intruder missions over the Continent. This machine, flown by Flight Lieutenant Karel Miroslav Kuttelwascher bears one of the first camouflage schemes destined for the "Intruders", with the codes painted red and the underside entirely black (Special Night) without any roundels. The pilot's personal insignia (the "Night Reaper") is only on the right.

Hawker Hurricane Mk IIC (BE581) from No 1 Squadron, Redhill, May , 1942. Pilot: Karel Miroslav "Kut" Kuttelwascher. He took part in the French Campaign with the French Air Force (GC III/6) before joining the RAF. The greatest Czech ace, the undisputed night intruder specialist, especially attacking German bombers on their return to base in France, his final score was 18 confirmed kills. His machine, the same as the above, was entirely painted black with a smaller sized tail flash.

Hawker Hurricane Mk IIC (NX864) from No 1 Squadron, Tangmere, England, September 1942. This squadron used Hurricane Mk IIs from January 1941 to September 1942, when they were replaced by Typhoons. A new camouflage scheme (Day Fighter Scheme), using two shades of grey and green with the code letters, fuselage stripe and propeller boss painted sky blue, appeared on the RAF fighters in the spring of 1941, the previous camouflage scheme being judged inappropriate for high altitudes.

Hawker Hurricane Mk IIC (Z2909) from No 1 Squadron, Redhill, England, May 1941. Lieutenant Jean Demozay obtained his third kill with this entirely black plane shooting down an He III during the night of 10-11 May 1941. Three days later he was promoted to command B Flight of No 1 Squadron. "Morlaix" (Demozay's code name in the FAFL – Free French Forces) ended the war with 18 conformed kills and two probables which made him the third French WWII ace.

Hawker Hurricane Mk IIC (Z3092) from No 3 Squadron, Stapleford Tawney, England, September 1941. No 3 was equipped with Hurricane Mk IIs from April 1941 to April 1943. This plane has been painted what was sometimes called the Interim Day Fighter Scheme, where the upper grey colour (Ocean Grey) of which there was not enough available when it was introduced, was replaced in the field by a similar shade obtained by mixing the grey used until then for the codes (medium sea grey) with black (Special Night) in the ratio 7 to 1.

Hawker Hurricane Mk IID (HV 663) from No 6 Squadron, Western Desert, Egypt, mid-1942. No 6 was only equipped with Hurricanes in May 1942 and specialised in ground attack operations and destroying enemy armour.

Hawker Hurricane Mk IID (BP554) from No 6 Squadron, Shandur, Egypt, April 1942. This squadron's Hurricane Mk IIDs turned out to be so effective when attacking the Afrika Korps' armour that they were quickly called the "Flying Can Openers".

Hawker Hurricane Mk IID (BP188) from No 6 Squadron, Western Desert, Egypt, mid-1942. No 6 was one of the rare squadrons to use Hurricanes only until the end of the war, its Mk IIs giving way to Mk IVs in 1944. The red propeller boss was one of the hallmarks of the Desert Air Force and was kept during the Italian Campaign.

Hawker Hurricane Mk IIB (BE171) from No 17 Squadron, Mingdalon, Burma, February 1942. Pilot: Sergeant J. F. 'Tex" Barrick. This plane, one of the rare ones to be painted with the desert camouflage scheme in this theatre, was normally assigned to the CO of No 17 Squadron, Squadron Leader C. A. C. "Bunny" Stone, but it was also used by "Tex" Barrick, an American volunteer in the RAF and the scorer of five confirmed kills.

Hawker Hurricane Mk IIC (serial number unknown) from No 17 Squadron, Alipore, India, end of 1942. No XVII, sent to the Far East just before the Japanese attack, was given the job of defending Rangoon from January 1942. With Burma rapidly overrun by the Japanese, it fell back on India where it was reformed the following June. This squadron kept its Mk IIs until the beginning of 1944 when they were replaced by Spitfires. Apart from its sky blue undersides, the main feature of this plane was its white (or very light grey) individual letter.

Hawker Hurricane Mk IIC (BG802) from No 28 Squadron, Cox's Bazaar, Burma, 1943. At first equipped with Westland Lysanders as an Army Co-operation Unit, No XXVIII (AC) received its Hurricanes in December 1942 at Lahore, India, with which it carried out tactical recce missions in Burma. This machine, equipped with cameras installed in a fairing fitted under the fuselage, has an unusual fin flash and one of the panels has been replaced but not repainted.

Hawker Hurricane Mk II (BM985) from No 28 Squadron, Calcutta, India, July 1942. Several Hurricanes were modified in the field (cameras added and extra radio fitted for liaising with the ground forces), especially in the Middle East, for carrying out tactical recce missions, replacing the Lysanders which were thought to be too vulnerable. Officially designated Tactical Reconnaissance Mk II (Tac R II), most of them kept their armament. Used for nighttime missions, this machine, which has no radio mast, has been painted blue black (Bosun Blue).

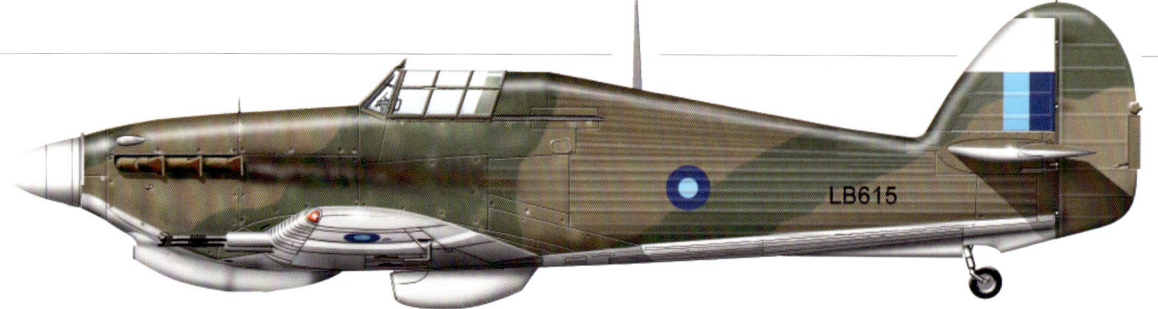

Hawker Hurricane PR Mk IIC (LB615) from No 28 Squadron, Cox's Bazaar, Burma, April 1944. This plane bears the British Far East markings with light grey under-surfaces, two-colour roundels and the South East Asia Air Command markings (white flashes on the wings, tails and elevators). Used for photoreconnaissance this plane was armed with two cannon instead of four.

Hawker Hurricane Mk IIC (BP589) from No 30 Squadron, Dambulla, Ceylon, December 1942. No 30 Squadron received its Mark IICs in March 1942 when in North Africa. Sent in an emergency to Ceylon to protect the island from Japanese attacks, most of the machines retained their desert camouflage schemes, at least to begin with.

Hawker Hurricane Mk IIC (LE336) from No 34 Squadron, Palel, India, end of 1943. Equipped earlier with Blenheim Mk IVs, No 34 received its Hurricane Mk IICs in April 1943 and used them as fighter-bombers in Burma from the following November onwards. The Azure or Light Mediterranean Blue covering the undersides is not the regulation colour; it ought to have been light grey (Medium Sea Grey).

Hawker Hurricane Mk IIC (LB836) from No 34 Squadron, Cox's Bazaar, Burma, 1945. The European camouflage (Day Fighter Scheme) was worn by new Hurricanes sent to the Far East and not repainted on the spot. Only the nationality markings were adapted to this theatre, without any red.

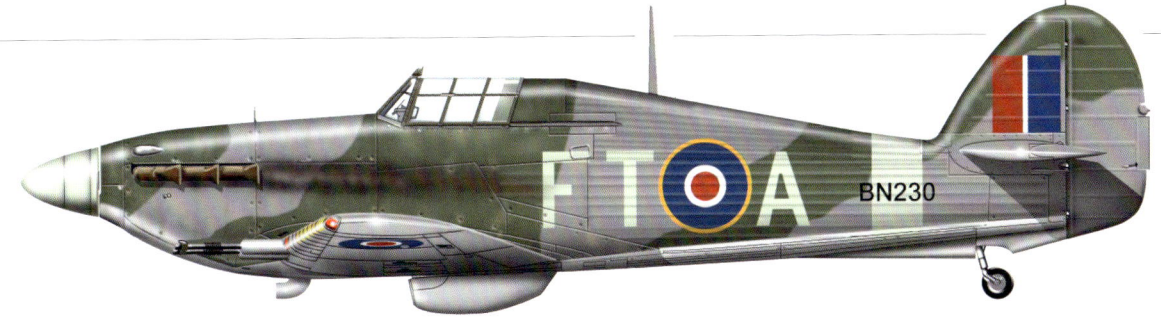

Hawker Hurricane Mk IIC (BN230) from No 43 Squadron, Tangmere, England, August 1942. Pilot: Squadron Leader Daniel "Danny" Le Roy du Vivier. This Dutch-born Belgian joined the RAF after his country capitulated. Incorporated into No 43 Sqn, he participated in part of the Battle of Britain and was sent to North Africa with his unit in September 1942. He finished the war as Wing Commander with three kills to his credit.

Hawker Hurricane Mk IIA (Z3150) from No 43 (China-British) Squadron, Tangmere, England, June 1942. After training pilots in the North following the Battle of Britain, No 43 resumed its operations over France when it returned to its base at Tangmere.

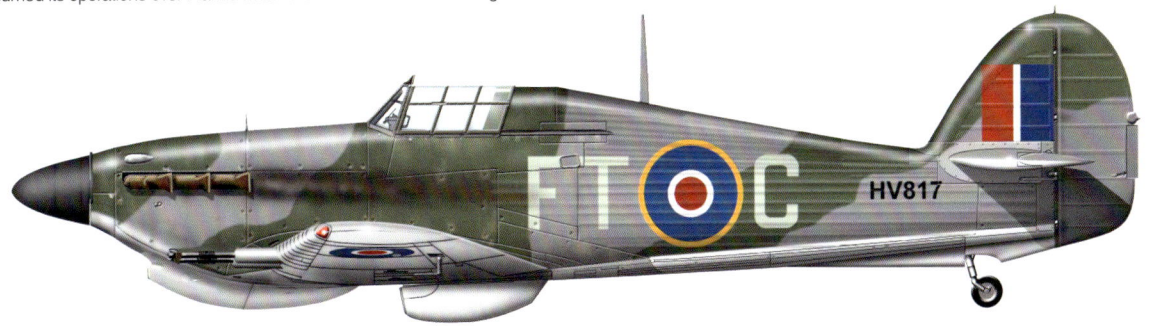

Hawker Hurricane Mk IIC (HV817) from No 43 Squadron, Alger-Maison Blanche, Algeria, November 1942. This squadron was sent to North Africa via Malta in September 1942 at the same time as it began re-equipping with only Hurricanes. As can be seen, the first machines used in the Tunisian Campaign retained their original camouflage scheme.

Hawker Hurricane Mk IIC (BD930) from No 73 Squadron, El Gamil, Egypt, October 1941. Sent to Egypt during the Battle of Britain, this squadron was given the task of defending the Suez Canal Zone before taking part in the war in the Western Desert. Like several units of the Desert Air Force its Hurricanes bore a stylised version of their insignia.

Hawker Hurricane Mk IIB (Z2633) from No 79 Squadron, Fairwood Common, England, end of 1941. Based in Wales after the Battle of Britain and given the task of defending the Midlands, No 79 received MK IIs at the beginning of 1942 and then left for India in June the same year.

Hawker Hurricane Mk IIC (BE500) from No 87 (United Provinces) Squadron, Warmwell, England, August 1942. Pilot: Squadron Leader Dennis Graham Smallwood. Used during the Dieppe Raid in August 1942, this plane was entirely repainted Special Night (black). Under the canopy, on the left only, there is the Squadron Leader's pennant and a cartouche with the words "United Provinces" surmounting the nickname Cawnpore. Faced with very heavy flak and forced to operate at low altitude, the Hurricane units engaged in Operation Jubilee (the abortive Dieppe Raid) suffered heavy losses.

Hawker Hurricane Mk IIC (serial number unknown) from No 87 Squadron, Warmwell, England, beginning of 1942. This plane which bears a variant (applied in the field) of the new camouflage scheme introduced in 1942, has its under surfaces painted black, the most appropriate colour for the night intruder missions to which the squadron was assigned from March 1941 to November 1942.

Hawker Hurricane Mk IIC (BP389) from No 94 Squadron, El Gamil, Egypt, mid-1942. Partly equipped with Curtiss Kittyhawks this squadron, specialising in ground attack, used only its Hurricane IICs for ground attack after May 1942, mainly for protecting convoys supplying the British Eighth Army.

Hawker Hurricane Mk IIB (Z3427) from No 121 (Eagle) Squadron, Kirton in Lindsy, England, July 1941. The second "Eagle Squadron" (made up of American volunteers) was formed in May 1941 and only used its Hurricanes until the end of the same year. When these units were transferred to the USAAF in September 1942, No 121 became the 355th Fighter Squadron of the 4th Fighter Group.

Hawker Hurricane Mk IIB (BD776) from No 128 Squadron, Hastings, Sierra Leone, end of 1942. No 128 was formed in October 1941 at Hastings, a base near Freetown in Sierra Leone, to protect the country from the threat of French forces stationed at Dakar in Senegal. When the threat disappeared, the unit was disbanded in March 1943. This machine which certain sources mention as painted with the "temperate land scheme" camouflage (brown and green) was used among others by Sergeant Arthur Todd and Squadron Leader John Ignatius "Iggy" Kilmartin.

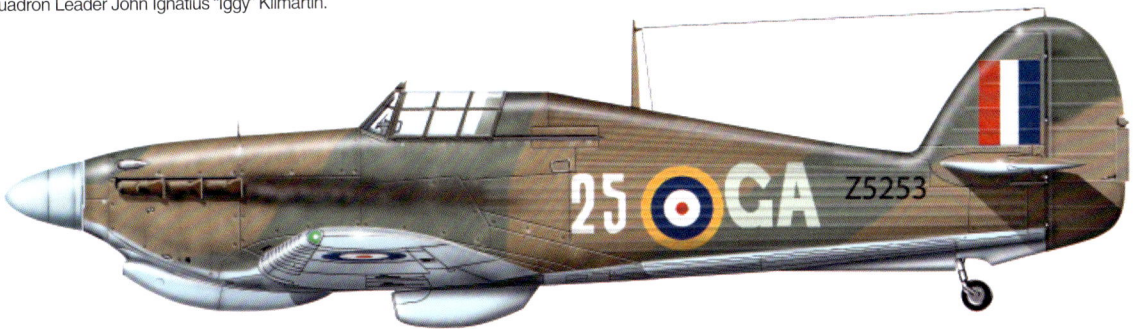

Hawker Hurricane Mk IIB (Z5253) from No 134 Squadron, Vaenga, USSR, September 1941. This squadron was sent to Vaenga airfield near Murmansk on 7 September 1941 to train future Soviet Hurricane pilots. Its mission over, it returned to England at the end of the following month leaving its planes in the USSR. The Vaenga Hurricanes markings were unusual as only the first letter of the code ("GV") was retained followed by an individual letter and a white order number, painted in Cyrillic.

Hawker Hurricane Mk IIB (Z5659) from No 135 Squadron, Mingdalon, Burma, February 1942. Pilot: Pilot Officer Jack Storey, who shot down two Ki-27 Nates (plus two probables) on the same day (6 February 1942). This unit was first sent to India then to Rangoon in Burma, where it was almost wiped out within a few days. The underside of this machine has been painted light blue (sky blue).

Hawker Hurricane Mk IID (KX561) from No 164 (Argentina-British) Squadron, Middle Wallop, England, June 1943. Created in April 1942, this squadron received Spitfires in May but as it was converted into a fighter-bomber unit, replaced them with Hurricanes (Mk IIDs then Mk IVs) which it kept until the end of the conflict.

Hawker Hurricane Mk IIB (BE421) from No 174 (Mauritius) Sqn, Manston, England, May 1942. Used for fighter-bomber sweeps, this "Hurribomber" was lost on 2 June 1942. Having suffered heavy losses in this role, No 174, created in March 1942, received Typhoons a year later.

Hawker Hurricane Mk IIA (Z2402) from No 185 Squadron, Hal Far, Malta, May 1941. Formed on 27 April 1941 on Malta for its own defence, this squadron was converted to Spitfires less than a year later, in March 1942.

Hawker Hurricane Mk IIB (Z2961) from No 185 Squadron, Hal Far, Malta, August 1941. The Malta Hurricanes, like the Spitfires later on, had the most varied camouflage schemes, often adapted to the island's specific environment. Here the upper surfaces have been painted dark green and middle stone, with sky blue lower surfaces and an individual letter painted medium sea grey.

Hawker Hurricane PR Mk IIC (DG622) from No 208 Squadron, El Bassa, Palestine, November 1942. This machine with no radio mast was used for tactical nighttime reconnaissance with cameras housed under the fuselage in a protective fairing.

Hawker Hurricane Mk IIB (HL830) from No 208 Squadron, El Bassa, Palestine, November 1942. As with the above, this plane has been painted entirely bosun blue with light blue propeller boss and individual letter. After fighting in North Africa, No 208 took part in the Italian Campaign.

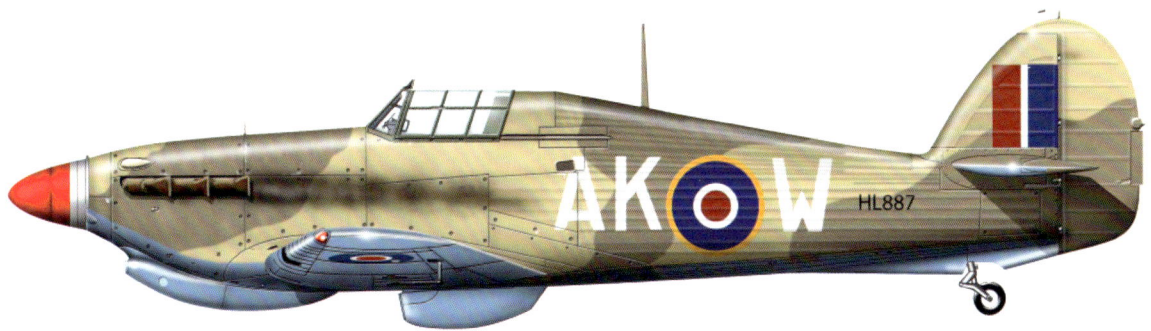

Hawker Hurricane Mk IIB (HL887) from No 213 (Ceylon) Squadron, Egypt, 1942. After being engaged in the Battle of Britain, this squadron was based in Egypt with detachments sent to Syria and Cyprus.

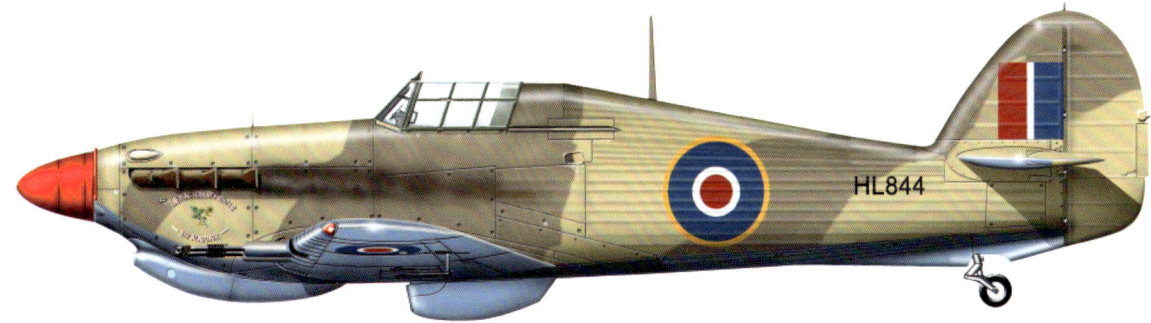

Hawker Hurricane Mk IIC (HL844) from No 237 (Rhodesia) Squadron, Kirkuk, Iraq, December 1942. No 237 was at first equipped with Gladiators and served in East Africa, as its name indicates. It received Hurricanes when it reached the Middle East. In 1942 it was sent to Iraq to defend the country against possible German raids from the Caucasus, this plane in particular being given the task of protecting oil wells in the Kirkuk region.

Hawker Hurricane Mk IIB (BP166) from No 238 Squadron, Egypt, 1942. This squadron, specialising in escort and ground attack operations, first flew Spitfires before receiving Hurricane Mk Is in June 1940, then Mk IIs when it transferred to North Africa at the end of 1941.

Hawker Hurricane Mk IIA (Z3663) from No 247 (China-British) Squadron, Predannack, England, August 1941. This squadron, flying Mk IIs from June 1941 to February 1943, remained stationed in England for the duration of the conflict which it finished flying Typhoon IBs.

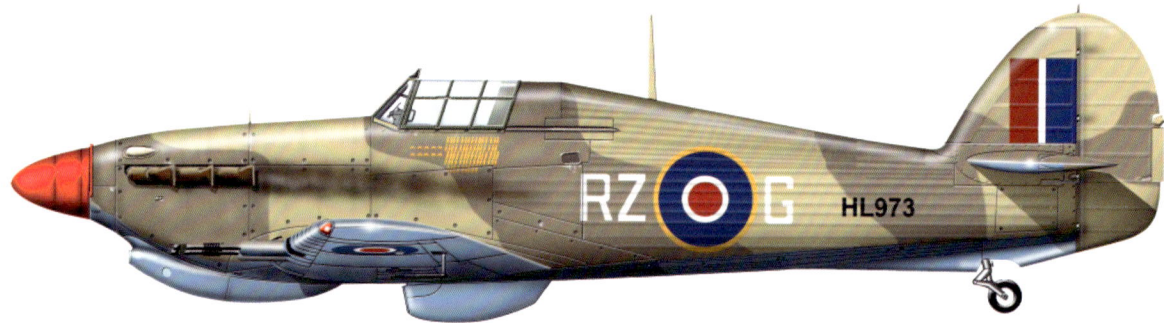

Hawker Hurricane Mk IIB (HL973) from No 241 Squadron, Souk-el-Khemis, Algeria, October 1943. First equipped with Lysanders then with Mustang Is and specialising in tactical reconnaissance and ground attack, this unit was sent to North Africa in November 1942 and received Spitfires in December 1943. This machine bears mission markings consisting of yellow vehicle and bomb silhouettes under the canopy on the left.

Hawker Hurricane Mk IIC (BD936) from No 247 (China-British) Squadron, Exeter, England, 1942. This plane, used for night intruder operations, has been painted entirely black (Special Night) and has smaller fuselage roundels covering the red codes, with the individual letter separated by a hyphen.

Hawker Hurricane Mk IIB (Z3971) from No 253 (Hyderabad State) Squadron, Highbaldstow, England, end of 1941. Before being sent to North Africa, No 253 was given the task of defending the Midlands, then the Orkneys. The code of this entirely black (Special Night) machine is medium sea grey with a nickname (Samastimas II) painted under the exhaust pipes on the left only.

Hawker Hurricane Mk IIB (BD701) from No 258 Squadron, Colombo Race-course, Ceylan, January 1942. It was shot down by a Mitsubishi A6M2 near Colombo on 5 April 1942. No 258, reformed in March 1942 in Ceylon, took part in the defence of the island against planes embarked aboard Japanese Navy aircraft carriers.

Hawker Hurricane Mk IIB (HL795) from No 274 Squadron, Battle of El Alamein, Egypt, end of 1942. The squadron was given the task of attacking enemy motorised columns and ships. The blue lightning flash painted around the fuselage roundel was the squadron's unofficial marking.

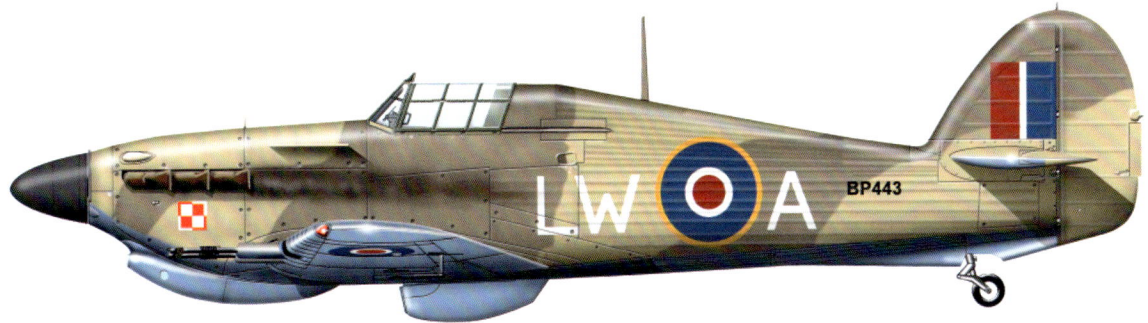

Hawker Hurricane Mk IIC (BP443) from No 318 (City of Gdansk) Squadron, Oassasin, Egypt, end of 1943. Created in March 1943, this squadron was made up of Polish personnel and pilots and was sent to the Middle East the following August to train there. At the end of this training, it was sent to support the 2nd Polish Army fighting in Italy.

Hawker Hurricane Mk IIB (BD930) from No 335 (Greek) Squadron, Dekheila, Egypt, September 1942. This unit was formed at Aqir with Greek personnel and pilots on 10 October 1941. To show its origins clearly, the individual letter was taken from the Greek alphabet (Sigma/S).

Hawker Hurricane Mk IIB (Z3658) from No 401 (Ram) Squadron, Digby, England, July 1942. No 1 Squadron RCAF was re-designated No 401 at Digby and incorporated into the RAF. It received its first Hurricanes at the end of 1940.

Hawker Hurricane Mk IIA (Z3230) from No 402 (Winnipeg Bears) Squadron, Digby, England, May 1941. No 2 Squadron RCAF became No 402 RAF in March 1942. After training for fighter-bomber missions which it carried out from November 1941 to March 1942, its pilots then received Spitfires.

Hawker Hurricane Mk IIB (BE485) from No 402 (Winnipeg Bears) Squadron, Warmwell, England, 1942. The squadron's "Hurribombers" were used for "Ramrod" missions (long distance bombing over the Continent) in France. Invisible from this angle, the individual letter has been copied under the forward cowling in small letters.

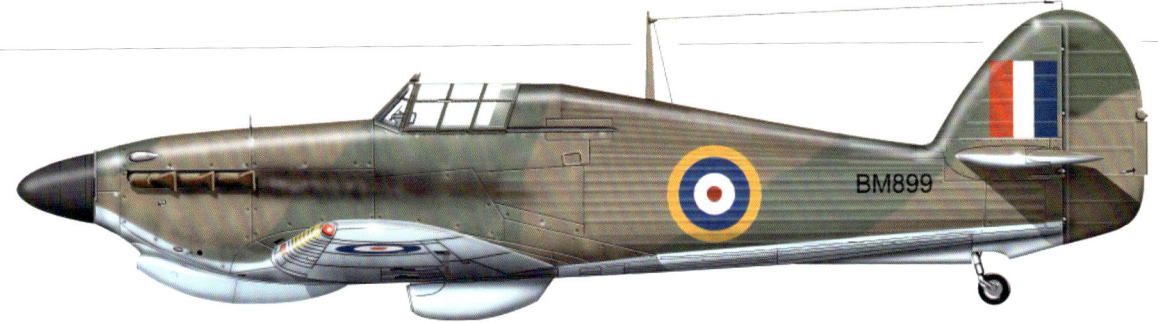

Hawker Hurricane Mk IIB (BM899) from No 488 (RNZAF) Squadron, Kallang, Singapore, end of January 1942. This Royal New Zealand Air Force squadron was formed in September 1941 and equipped with CAC Wirraways. After trying desperately to defend Singapore with Buffaloes, it went to Sumatra where it was overwhelmed by the Japanese again. The pilots therefore left their surviving planes to No 243 Squadron and sought refuge in Australia. Temperate land camouflage scheme on the upper surfaces but sky blue underneath.

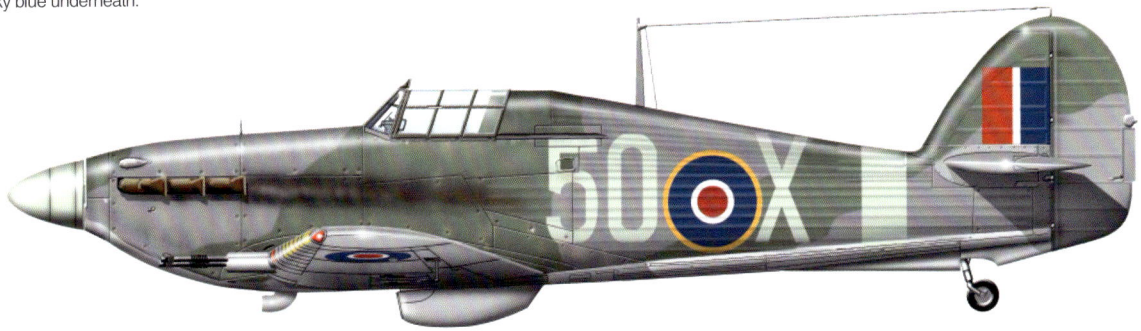

Hawker Hurricane Mk IIC (Met) (serial number unknown) from No 521 Squadron, Docking, England, September 1944. This unit, used for weather forecasting, was reformed at Docking in September 1943. Equipped with various types of machines, often unarmed, like this Hurricane, it supplied information for operational or rescue units. No 521 replaced its old Gladiators in September 1944 with Hurricanes which it held on to until February 1946.

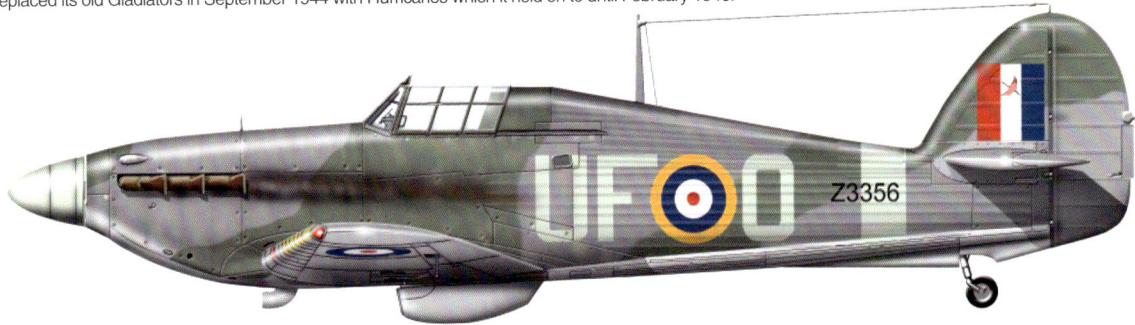

Hawker Hurricane Mk IIB (Z3356) from No 506 (County of London) Squadron, Northolt, England, July 1941. This Auxiliary Air Force squadron took part in the Battle of Britain and when in August 1941 it was given the task of trying out the Bell P-39 Aircobra, it gave up its Hurricanes which in the meantime had become Hurribombers.

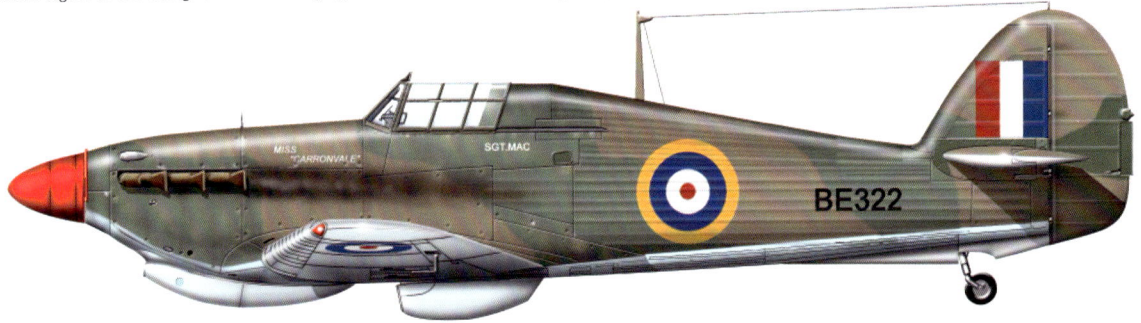

Hawker Hurricane Mk IIB (BE322) from No 605 (County of Warwick) Squadron, Tjilitan, Java, February 1942. Pilot: Sergeant J. MacIntosh. This Hurricane christened Miss Carronvale/Sergeant Mac, was a former No 248 Squadron machine abandoned by the unit in Java, No 605 using whatever planes were available for defending the island before being overwhelmed in turn and disbanded in February 1942.

Hawker Hurricane Mk II (Z2703) from No 615 (County of Surrey) Squadron, Kenley, England, May 1941. This Auxiliary Air Force squadron took part in the first phase of the Battle of Britain before being sent to rest in Scotland. Shipped to South East Asia it received its first Spitfires in October 1943. Note the large size code letters placed quite far forward on the fuselage

Hawker Hurricane PR Mk II (BH125) from No 3 (PRU) Squadron, Dum Dum, India, November 1942. This squadron, given photoreconnaissance tasks over Burma and Siam, used Hurricanes (PR IIs and Mk IICs) until the end of 1943 when it became No 285 Squadron. This plane, equipped with cameras in a ventral fairing, was entirely painted blue-black (Bosun blue), does not have any fuselage roundels and is unusual in that its fin flash has a white border.

Hawker Hurricane Mk X (AG162) from No 55 Operational Training Unit (OTU), Usworth, England, 1942. Intended for training Fighter Command pilots, this unit was equipped with Hurricanes and Miles Masters which had various fuselage codes.

Hawker Hurricane Mk IIB (HV498) from No 41 (SAAF) Squadron, Egypt, July 1942. Created in October and at first equipped with struck-off planes (Hawker Hartbees and Curtiss Mohawks), the South-African squadron started receiving its Hurricanes only in 1943 and in particular Mark IIBs when it transferred from Kenya to Egypt in April. Given the task of defending this country, its only combat operation was a sweep over Crete on 23 July 1943.

Hawker Hurricane Mk IIC (MW339) from No 1555 Flight of the Air Despatch Letter Service, Northolt, England, 1944. The ADLS' job was to take letters by air to the troops fighting in the front line, especially on the Continent following the Normandy landings.

Hawker Hurricane Mk IIC (LF380) from No 83 OTU, Peplow, England, June 1944. Given the task of training night-time bombers, this unit which didn't last very long (August 1943 to October 1944) was also equipped with unarmed Hurricanes most of the time, which sported the invasion stripes like all Allied aircraft at the time of the landings in Normandy.

Hawker Hurricane Mk IIA (Z5594), 1941. The planes linking Takoradi (Gold Coast – present-day Ghana) and Egypt were given white markings over the dorsal area and the tail in order to make them more visible in case they were forced to make an emergency landing, particularly in the desert. The number hastily painted on the fuselage is an order number used only for the transfer flight. This plane whose lower surfaces are sky blue, was assigned to No 274 Squadron in Egypt.

Hawker Hurricane Mk IIC (LF534) from 1688 Bomber Training Flight, Newmarket, England, April 1944. This unit's unarmed Hurricanes were used as "aggressors" for RAF bomber machine gunners.

Hawker Hurricane Mk IIA (Z2827) from the Night Fighting Unit, Ta' Qali, Malta, July 1941. This plane from the flight whose job was to defend the island at night was repainted in the field in a non-standard scheme with its lower surfaces painted black.

Hawker Hurricane Mk IIB (BG737) of the Malta Night Fighter Unit, Ta' Qali, Malta, July 1941. Belonging to the same unit as the above, this machine was painted entirely black, more appropriate to its nighttime missions. All the roundels are Type Bs, including the lower surfaces and the fuselage.

Hawker Hurricane Mk IIB (BM904) from an unknown squadron (No 605?) abandoned at Kallang, Singapore, February 1942. Quickly overwhelmed by the Japanese, the squadrons defending Singapore abandoned their machines before escaping to Indonesia. This plane was recovered in flying condition and subsequently tried out by the Japanese.

Hawker Hurricane Mk IIC (PZ865). The last Hurricane (the 14 533rd!) to come off the production line in the summer of 1944 bears the inscription the "Last of the Many". It was almost immediately bought up by Hawker and used for promotional purposes and as a test machine. After being used in competitions in the fifties and taking part in the film, the Battle of Britain, in 1968, it was finally given to the Memorial Flight, an association which keeps it in flying condition, in 1972. In 2010 it took part in various meetings in England bearing the colours of the Czech ace, Karel Kuttelwascher.

Hawker Hurricane Mk IIC (PZ865), the "Last of the Many" took part in the 1950 King's Cup Air Race, put in by Princess Margaret and flown by Group Captain Peter Townsend, the Battle of Britain air ace. Painted entirely royal blue and registered "G-AMAU", it won second place. It kept this livery until the end of the year before being camouflaged and used as a service plane by Hawker's before being given to the Memorial Flight.

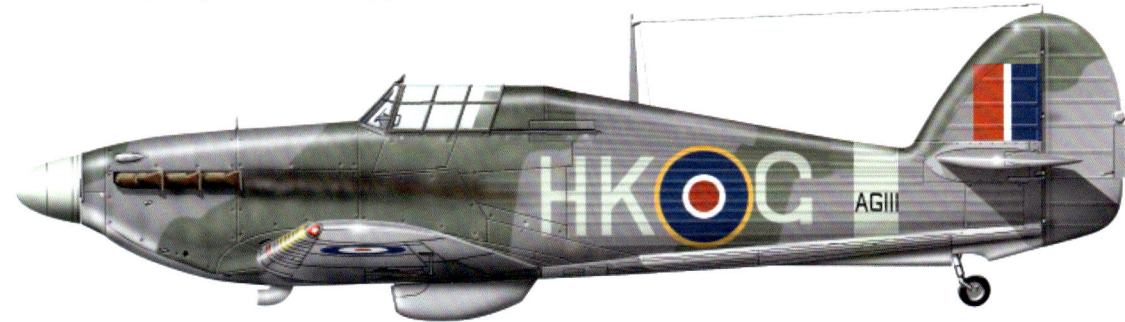

Hawker Hurricane Mk X (AG111) from the Fighter Leaders School, Millfield, England, January 1944. This school specialised in training unit leaders and was short-lived – January to October 1944. The Hurricane Mk X was only a Mk II produced in Canada and was identical externally.

Hawker Hurricane Mk XII (JS290) from No 527 Squadron, Digby, England, 1945. Another second line unit, No 527's job was radar calibration using Hurricanes from June 1943 to April 1945 including Mk XIIs made in Canada like this one, replacing the twin-engined Blenheims.

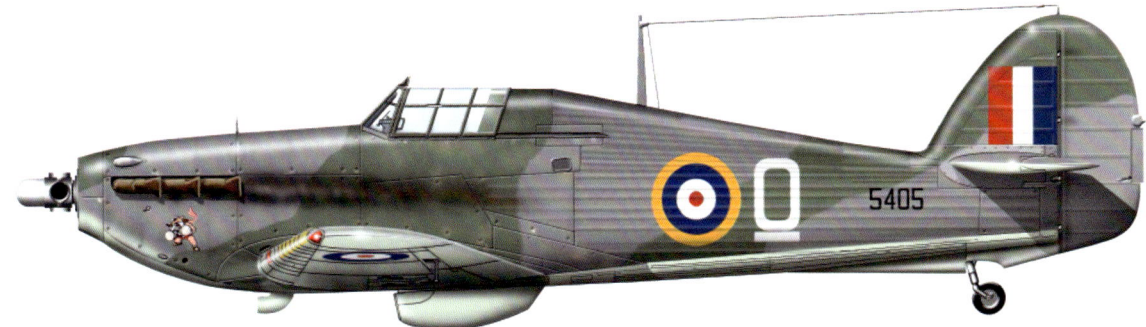

Hawker Hurricane Mk XII (5405) from No 135 Squadron RCAF, Patricia Bay, British Columbia, Canada, 1942. This plane whose squadron was given the task of protecting Alaska, crashed near its base on 4 February 1942. Damaged beyond repair, it was used for spare parts and scrapped at the end of the war.

Above.
The second Hurricane Mk IIE prototype, later re-designated Mk IV, powered by a Merlin 27 fitted with a three-bladed propeller.

THE HURRICANE MARK IV

ON **14 MARCH 1943** the prototype of a new Hurricane version took to the air, the Mark IIE. As the designation clearly indicates, this was in fact just a further development of the plane, specially designed for ground attack, with improved protection for the forward part (extra armour around the engine, the cockpit and the radiator) and a universal wing (or "E"[1]), which could carry all sorts of loads, rockets, drop tanks, bombs or cannon, without modifying the electrical circuits and the fuel pipes. This prototype (in fact a Mark II – serial number KX405 – taken directly off the production lines at the Langley factory) was at first provisionally fitted with a Merlin 32 driving a Rotol four-bladed propeller while waiting for the Merlin 27 intended for the this version to be available. The latter developed 1 620 bhp on take off and was specially tuned to work in hot climates (it was in fact a "tropicalised" version of the Merlin XX) and low altitudes, driving a Rotol RS 5/11 three-bladed propeller.

Less than a week after this first flight, on 23 March 1943, a second prototype (6KZ193) was fitted with the originally planned engine and a three-bladed propeller and in turn took to the air and the two machines, armed with two 40-mm cannon housed in underwing gondolas went through a series of trials.

Outwardly similar to the Mk IID (increased pilot and engine protection, and a slightly bigger radiator), the new plane was finally re-designated Mark IV[2] after the 270th example came off the production lines; it turned out to be much more effective in a hostile environment (intense AA fire) than the IID; and above all, it was much less vulnerable than the Spitfire, Mustang and Typhoon which were indeed faster and more agile because they carried less armour, but which were more vulnerable to ground fire, in particular because of their liquid cooling system which was much less well protected.

---

1. The "A" wing was fitted the eight .303 machine guns, the "B" had twelve and the "C" was armed with four 20-mm cannon.
2. The designation Mark III had been intended originally for planes equipped with Merlins made under licence in the US by Packard and in the end was not used.

Opposite.
Mk IID "BP173" was used for weapon trials at the A&AEE, Boscombe Down, in July 1942 before being transformed into a Mark IV.

Above.
Hurricane MK IV from No 151 Operational Training unit (OTU) at Peshawar, India after the war. The plane has been entirely painted aluminium and has small diameter SEAC-type roundels on the fuselage and the wings.

Built from April 1943 to September 1944 at the same time as the Hurricane Mk IIC (a ratio of one Mk IV to ten Mk IIs), the 524 Mk IV examples produced were used by the RAF in the Mediterranean, Far East and in Europe, with deliveries reaching operational units in May 1943.

The Hurricane Mk IV's main armament quickly became the 3-inch rocket (Rocket Projectile or RP) which in the end was used more than the 40-mm cannon. Each wing was fitted with four rails to which the rockets were attached, with a plate for protecting the underwing surface during firing. The first trials with this weapon had been carried out in October 1941 on a Hurricane Mk I fitted with only three rails under each wing, then on two Mk IIs. The RP was a cheap, rudimentary weapon comprising a steel tube containing solid fuel for the rocket and guided by cross-shaped fins. The explosive was in a screw-on head at the front. There were three types of rockets: 25 lb for armour, 60 lb semi-armour-piercing and 25 lb steel ones for training. The rockets, fired two at a time or in salvoes, were not very accurate since aiming them was very rudimentary but their destructive power was nonetheless very effective and at the time no armour could withstand them – a distinct advantage over the 20-mm cannon usually used.

The Hurricane Mk IV often carried "asymmetrical" armament, i.e. rockets (four under one wing) and a drop tank, one 40-mm canon in a fairing or a bomb, depending on the missions (under the other). When the cannon were used, two .303 machine guns were kept, as on the Mk IIC or D, in order to help aiming, using tracer bullets. The planes, loaded with rockets and heavily protected, were clearly slow and not very manoeuvrable, but they excelled in the ground attack (destroying buildings, vehicle concentrations – armoured or otherwise) and even anti-shipping strike roles.

Operational use

The Hurricane Mk IV was used by eleven front-line squadrons: seven based in Great Britain, two in Italy and two in Burma. This version was put into service naturally in the units stationed in Great Britain first, in May-June 1943 but its operational use in this theatre was short-lived. Nos 164 and 184 Squadrons received their Mk IIDs in May 1943 and used them with the 2nd TAF (Tactical Air Force) in the ground attack – especially the V-1 launch sites installed on the continent – and the anti-shipping roles until March 1944 when they were replaced by Typhoons.

In No 137 Squadron – one of the few Westland Whirlwind-equipped squadrons – the Mk IV's career was even shorter since they were put into service in July 1943, and replaced in January the following year. As for the other four squadrons (Nos 185 RAF and 438, 439 and 440 RCAF), they spent such a short time in their units, sometimes not even a month, that they weren't even used operationally... Once it had been replaced in the front line in the West, the Hurricane Mk IV continued to be used for service missions like radar calibration or anti-aircraft defence, or even as "postmen", for rapid mail delivery for the troops in Normandy.

No 6 Squadron, a forerunner in the use of Hurricanes for ground attack, was given its first Mk IVs in July 1943 while still based in North Africa using them intensively in Italy from February 1944 as

SPECIFICATIONS HURRICANE MARK IV

Type: Single seat fighter-bomber
Powerplant: One V-12 liquid-cooled Rolls Royce Merlin 24 rated at 1 620 bhp on take-off.
Dimensions
Length: 32 ft 3 in (9,84 m)
Height: 13 ft 1 in (3,99 m)
Wingspan: 40 ft (12,19 m)
Wing Surface: 257.990 sq ft (23,97 m^2)
Weight (empty): 5 533 lb (2 515 kg)
Weight (fully laden): 8 460 lb (3 832 kg)

Performances
Maximum speed: 332 mph (531 km/h)
Maximum range: 443 miles (708 km) (956 miles (1 530 km) with two 44-Imp gallon (200 l) drop tanks)
Operational Ceiling: 32 475 ft (9 900 m)
Armament
Two 40-mm Vickers S cannon, two Browning .303 (7.7 mm) machine guns, two 250 lb or 500-lb bombs (110 or 230 kg), eight RP-3 60-lb rockets.

Above.
Another view of Mk IV "BP 173" fitted with eight underwing rockets.

well as in the Balkans supporting Tito's Yugoslav partisans and also in Greece, Cyprus and the Adriatic, especially against shipping. This squadron, the only one equipped with this version to remain in this theatre until the arrival of No 351 (Yugoslav) Squadron in September 1944, used its planes to develop new tactics, often attacking its targets in a half-dive, sometimes taking advantage of the moonlight. It kept its machines for a further eighteen months after the end of the war, only replacing them with Hawker Tempest Mk VIs in 1947. In Burma only two squadrons received Mk IVs in 1943[3], planes which were indeed "tropicalised" (with an extra filter) but camouflaged for the European theatre of operations, i.e. grey and green, with only the roundels being adapted for the Far East (by having the red removed). As in the Mediterranean, the Mk IV in the Far East was the only Allied plane to be equipped with 40-mm cannon[4] and for that reason, it was a considerable support for the ground troops against the Japanese in often very difficult conditions. No 20 Squadron received its first Hurricanes in January 1943 then replaced them in May with Mk IIDs which, because of the lack of canon shells, were used mainly for tactical recce missions. In December one of the flights (A Flight) converted to Hurricane IVs and used them alongside the earlier versions, armed mainly with rockets, until the end of the war in September 1945. As for No 42 Squadron, the second unit using Mk IVs, it swapped its Blenheims for this model in December 1943 and used them until they were replaced by Thunderbolts in June 1945.

The Hurricane Mark V

Intended from the outset for the war in the Far East and especially in Burma where the Mk IID was already engaged, the next version of the Hurricane, armed with 40-mm cannon was logically the Mark V. Its "prototype" was none other than that for the Mk IIE/Mk IV, KX405, powered by a Merlin 32 which could be pushed up to 1 700 bhp at low altitudes and which drove a four-bladed propeller. This machine took to the air for the first time on 3 April 1943. Able to fly at 328 mph (525 km) at 500 feet (150 m) with a 9 284 lb (4 220 kg) load and armed with two 40-mm cannon, this model was not produced in series in the end – only a second prototype (NL255) was built, because the Air Ministry thought its performances inadequate[5] and especially because large numbers of the previous versions (IIC, IID and IV) were still available in India.

---

3. *The other RAF front line squadrons equipped with Hurricanes (mainly Mk IIDs) in the Far East were Nos 11, 34, 60 and 113.*
4. *The P-51 Mustang could also carry rockets but its fixed armament comprised only machine guns, like the P-47 Thunderbolt, though the Typhoon "only" had (four) 20-mm cannon.*
5. *The Mk V flew as fast as the Mk I but it was 50% heavier!.*

Hurricane Mark IV

Hawker Hurricane Mk IIE (KZ193). This is the second prototype of this version, later re-designated Mark IV, which was powered by the standard engine (Merlin 27) driving a three-bladed propeller, the first prototype being powered by a Merlin 32 with a four-bladed propeller. Outwardly similar to the Mk II, the Mk IV differed by its radiator which had been enlarged to improve cooling at low altitudes, a feature which was fitted later onto the Mk II used in the ground attack role.

Hawker Hurricane Mk IV (KZ188) from No 6 Squadron, Prkos (Yugoslavia), April 1945. No 6 Squadron kept its Hurricanes until the end of the war and was one of the few units to deploy the Mark IV en masse on the Western Front, in Italy and in the Balkans from February 1944.

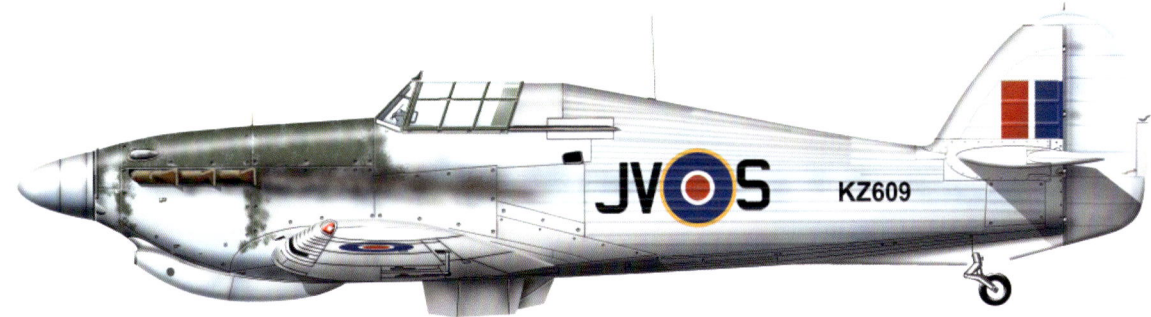

Hawker Hurricane Mk IV (KZ609) from No 6 Squadron, Nicosia (Cyprus), 1946. After the war, it was used for service and training missions and was entirely repainted aluminium. This paint wore off, quickly allowing the original camouflage to re-appear, especially on the most exposed spots.

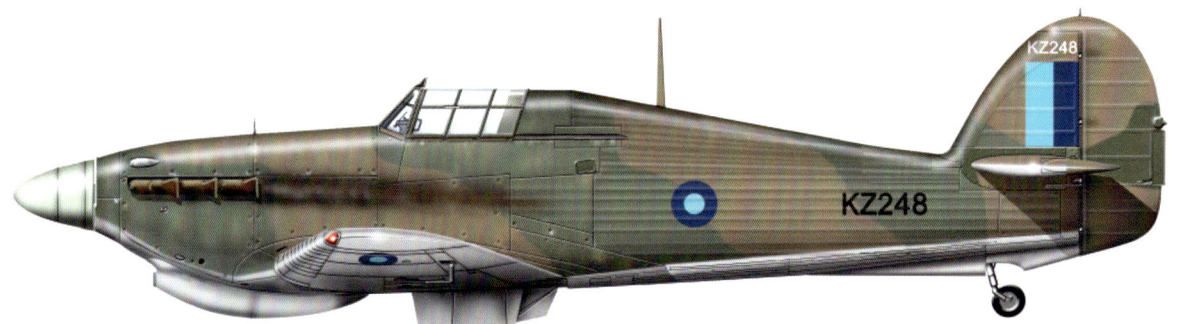

Hawker Hurricane Mk IV (KZ248) from No 28 Squadron, Kuala Lumpur (Malaysia), 1946. Still in use after the end of the war, this plane kept its South East Asia (SEA) camouflage scheme of dark earth and dark green on the upper surfaces, and medium sea grey on the lower surfaces. The small diameter, two-colour roundels (18 inches) were worn in the usual six places.

Hurricane Mark IV

Hawker Hurricane Mk IV from No 42 Squadron, Onbauk (Burma), 1944. This squadron carried out ground attack operations (Rhubarb) when it received its IICs at the end of 1943 and carried on with these operations after it converted to Mk IVs in May the following year, until it was (temporarily) disbanded, in May 1945.

Hawker Hurricane Mk IV (KZ944) from No 42 Squadron, Meiktila (Burma), July 1945. This squadron re-formed in June 1945 with elements of No 146, was equipped with Thunderbolts, with the Hurricanes still in service being used for training and liaison, and repainted entirely in aluminium.

Hawker Hurricane Mk IV (LD345) from No 60 Squadron, Mingaladon (Burma), May 1945. For the most part equipped with Mk IICs, this ground attack squadron fought in support of the British 14th Army, and also received rocket-armed Mk IVs.

Hawker Hurricane Mk IV (KX561) from No 164 (Argentina-British) Squadron, Fairlop (Great Britain), end of 1943. Given ground attack missions in preparation for the Normandy landings, in March 1944 No 164 replaced its Hurricanes, among which were the Mk IVs received in September 1943, with Typhoons.

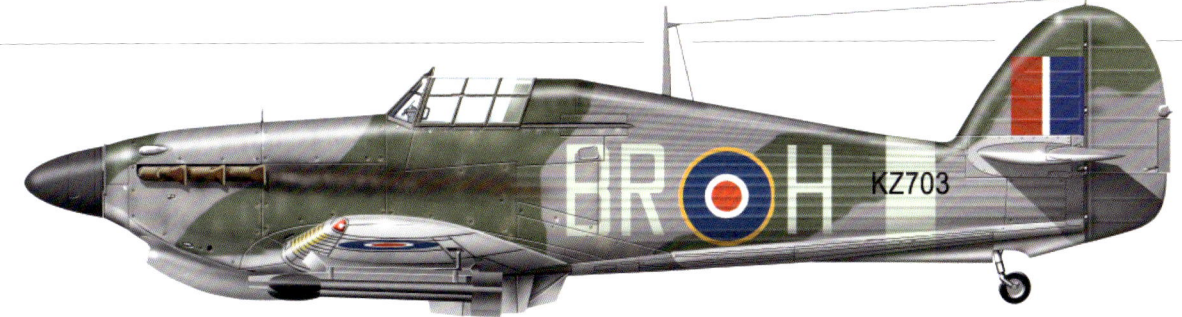

Hawker Hurricane Mk IV (KZ703) from No 184 Squadron. This squadron was allocated a number of targets in France, especially the V-1 launch sites, until the beginning of 1944, when its Hurricanes were replaced by Typhoons.

Hawker Hurricane Mk IV (KZ576) from No 288 Squadron, Collyweston (Great Britain). Equipped with various types of aircraft, this unit trained the AA gunners in Yorkshire and Lincolnshire by simulating air raids. It gave up its Hurricanes (Mk Is, IICs and Mk IVs) in November 1944.

Hawker Hurricane Mk IV (LF468) from No 351 (Yugoslav) Squadron, Isle of Vis (Yugoslavia), December 1944. Two squadrons (Nos 351 and 352) made up of Yugoslav personnel and pilots were formed in North Africa in 1944 and carried out ground attack missions for the Yugoslav National Liberation Army in the Balkans in October 1944, attached to 281 Wing of the RAF's Balkan Air Force. The planes bore their national colours after 1944, these markings being inspired by the RAF's on which a red star was painted. Apart from its score painted under the exhaust pipes, this plane was christened "Marko Oreskovic", after one of the Yugoslav partisans killed by the Chetniks in 1941 and declared "Yugoslav People's Hero" in 1945.

Hawker Hurricane Mk IV (LD570) from No 439 (Westmount) Squadron, Ayr (Great Britain), January 1944. Formed in October 1941, N°123 Squadron RCAF was chosen to serve overseas and arrived in Great Britain in January 1944 where it was re-designated No 439 Squadron. It only kept its Hurricanes for a few weeks since it converted to Typhoons the following February.

Hurricane Aces

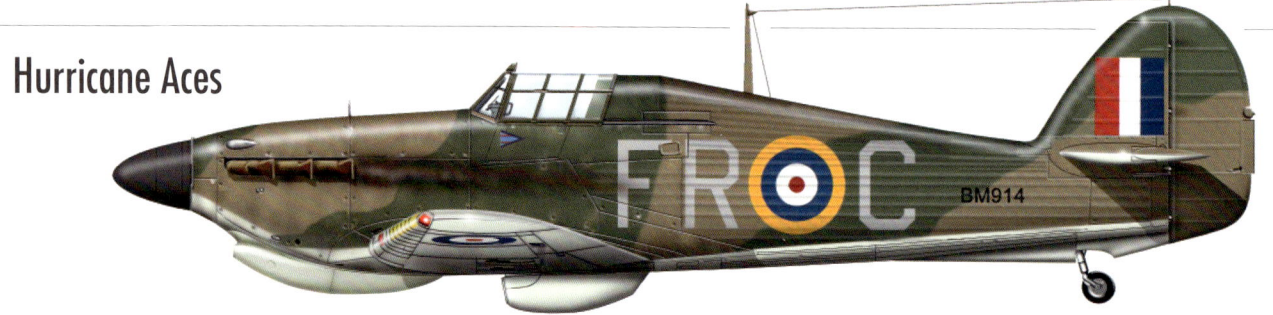

Hawker Hurricane Mk IIB (BM914) from No 267 Wing, Mingaladon, Burma, beginning of 1942. Pilot: Wing Commander Frank Reginald CARREY, 29 kills (or 28 according to the sources), all won with Hurricanes. This plane was one of two used by "Chota" Carrey while he commanded this wing in Burma; it uses the pilot's initials as its markings.

Hawker Hurricane Mk I Trop (AS 988) from No 33 Squadron, Crete, beginning of 1941; pilot: Marmaduke St-John PATTLE, 26 kills aboard Hurricanes (out of a total of 41, or even 60 according to some sources!). "Pat" Pattle who began his career on Gloster Gladiators in No 80 Squadron in August 1940 was the Commonwealth's Ace of Aces during WWII. A remarkable fighter pilot (his tally includes, among others, seven Bf 109Es and three Bf 110s), appointed No 33 Squadron's CO in March 1941, he was shot down trying to help his partner on 20 April 1941 near Eleusis, in Greece.

Hawker Hurricane Mk I (V7357) from No 501 (County of Gloucester) Squadron, Kenley, England, September 1940. Pilot: James Harry LACEY, 23 kills on Hurricanes (28 in all). "Ginger" Lacey, the top scorer of the Battle of Britain was sent to the Far East where he scored his last kill (a Ki-43 Hayabusa) on 19 February 1945. After flying the first Spitfire to fly over Japan, he continued his career with the RAF after the conflict.

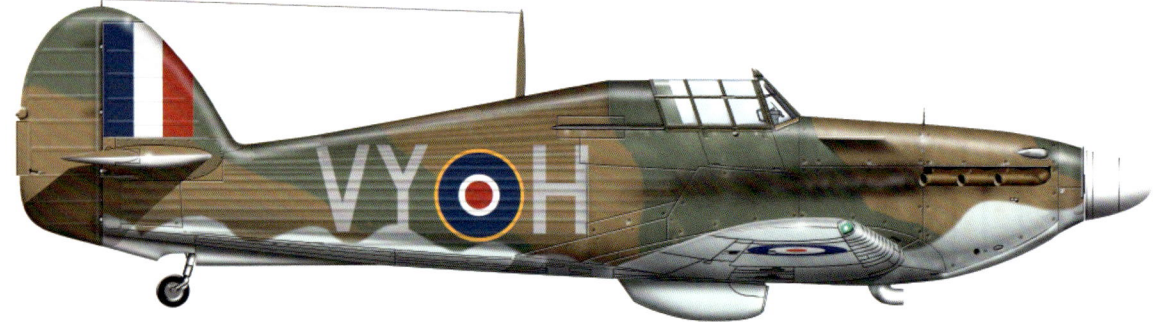

Hawker Hurricane Mk I (serial number unknown) from No 85 Squadron, Kirton in Lindsey, England, end of 1940. Pilot: Geoffrey ALLARD, 23 kills, all obtained with Hurricanes. After obtaining his first successes over France in No 85 Sqn, "Sammy" Allard was awarded the DFM in May 1940 and the DFC two months later. After shooting down a Bf 109 and a Do 17 on 1 September 1940, his last kills, he was killed on 13 March 1941 during a test flight.

Hawker Hurricane Mk I (P3144) from No 32 (The Royal) Squadron, Biggin Hill, England, July 1940. Pilot: Michael Nicholson CROSSLEY, 22 kills, all on Hurricanes. This plane was also used by Sqn. Ldr. J. Worrall. After scoring his first kill on 18 May 1940, "Mike" (or "Red Knight") Crossley was made No 32 Sqn's Squadron Leader the following July and scored his 22nd and last kill on 25 August putting his squadron in the lead for the number of kills obtained during the Battle of Britain. He then left for the United States where he became a test pilot with the British Air Commission.

Hawker Hurricane Mk I (Z3150) from No 43 (China British) Squadron, Drem, England, May 1941. Pilot: Flight Lieutenant Frederick DALTON-MORGAN, 22 kills. After distinguishing himself during the Battle of Britain, "Tommy" (or "Butch") Dalton-Morgan, a descendant of the famous buccaneer Henry Morgan, and when his squadron converted into a night-fighter unit, he made several kills in this new role.

Hawker Hurricane Mk I (L1630) from No 87 Squadron, Lille-Seclin, France, May 1940. Pilot: Pilot Officer William Denis DAVID, 20 kills, all on Hurricane. This machine was abandoned in France when British troops retreated in June 1940. David, one of the French Campaign aces, carried on with his career on Hurricanes after October 1940, when he joined No 213 Squadron, which was then sent to the Middle East in 1941.

Hawker Hurricane Mk I (P3308) from No 605 (County of Warwick) Squadron, Crowdon, England, September 1940. Pilot: Archibald Ashmore MacKELLAR, 20 kills (21, according to certain sources), all on Hurricanes. "Archie" MacKellar was the first British pilot to have shot down a German plane (an He 111) over England. On 7 October 1940 he shot down five Messerschmitt Bf 109Es in less than ten minutes, which earned him a DFC and a DSO. He died in rather unclear circumstances during his last dogfight over Redhill with his attacker, a Bf 109, also being his last victim.

Because of space, we have not represented the third and final pilot who won 20 victories aboard Hurricane, Herbert James Lampriere « Darkie » HALLOWES, from No 43 Squadron, whose usual aircraft (Mk I serial N2585) was coded FT°U.

Above.
Filling up a Sea Hurricane Mk IB on the deck of HMS Argus. This aircraft carrier, launched at the end of the Great War resumed its training status after taking part in Operation Torch, the Allied landings in North Africa. (IWM)

THE SEA HURRICANE

JUST BEFORE THE NORWEGIAN CAMPAIGN, at the beginning of 1940, Hawker envisaged transforming the Hurricane into a seaplane by fitting two floats, those originally intended for the Blackburn Roc. The project was quickly abandoned but the question of disposing of a version of the plane which was specially adapted to shipping and the sea, and used for protecting ships arose again in the summer of 1940 when the Germans settled down on the coast of newly occupied France and were thereby able to dispatch aircraft more easily to harass Allied sea lanes.

Great Britain could only rely on the convoys sent from North America for its supplies and as England cruelly lacked aircraft carriers at the time (HMS Courageous and HMS Glorious were lost at the beginning of the war), there were none available to protect the convoys on the high seas. In the emergency, and while waiting for the first escort carriers to be delivered it was decided to carry out recce missions with planes catapulted from specially equipped ships.

The Sea Hurricane Mk IA and the CAMs

At first, five Fighter Catapult Ships (FCS)[1] on which a catapult had been erected were given a Fairey Fulmar which was launched with a single rocket. But as this two-seat fighter turned out to be too slow for intercepting the enemy, it was decided to replace it with modified Hurricanes withdrawn from service by Fighter Command to equip a new kind of ship – the Catapult Aircraft Merchantmen (CAM).

Called the Sea Hurricane Mk IA[2] these planes were only different because of their specific Royal Navy radio equipment, their reinforced fuselage, stowing rings and the inevitable catapult braces. Their use was quite unusual in that they could only be used once. Indeed unless operating within range of the coast where they could land after their mission, the pilots of these planes[3] which were catapulted as soon as the enemy was detected[4], had no choice but to ditch or bale out as near to a "friendly" ship as possible and be picked up… In order to increase their range slightly, some of the machines were fitted with extra 44-gallon drop tanks and the pilot's comfort was improved, especially for those operating in the freezing waters of the North Atlantic, by installing a system so that they could wear heated boots and gloves, with the cockpit also being heated.

The first time a "Hurricat" (or a "Catafighter" as these fighters were quickly dubbed) was used from an FCS was on 2 August 1941 in the South Atlantic, off Sierra Leone when one of them managed to shoot down an Fw 200 Condor, the pilot being recovered without hitch.

As for the first time it was used from a CAM, this took place on 1 November 1941, when SS Empire Foam launched its plane against a marauding Fw 200.

In all 35 CAM ships were modified[5], six being used for North Atlantic convoy duty until July 1943. As for the pilots, who were volunteers, and the maintenance crews, all were specially trained at the Merchant Ship Fighter Unit (MSFU) at Speke, near Liverpool. Each team aboard a CAM comprised a pilot (two for the USSR or Mediterranean convoys) and five specialists whose job was to ope-

---

1. The FCSs were designated under the term "Pegasus Class". Three of them (Ariguani, Maplin and Patia, sunk in 1941) were former cruise ships, whereas one of them was a former seaplane carrier (Pegasus) and the last an anti-aircraft cruiser (Springbank, sunk in September 1941); the first victorious Hurricat belonged to one of them (Maplin).
2. The name Sea Hurricane Mk I – or even just Sea Hurricane – was at first given to machines bought by the Royal Navy and used by three of its squadrons, Nos 811, 807 and 808. Only the latter used them operationally, from land bases in Palestine. These planes were absolutely identical to the RAF Mk Is; their name only designated their owners.
3. Each CAM carried a single Sea Hurricane, on permanent standby (engine warmed up regularly, pilot at action stations when the alert was given) as soon as the ship entered a danger zone.
4. Catapulting (with retracted undercarriage) was carried out using two 2-in rockets enabling the plane to reach the speed of 60 knots (69 mph/111 kph) in 80 feet (25 m)
5. Eight private ships were requisitioned, two were lost in action. The other twenty-seven were "Empire Ships", belonging to the Ministry of War Transport. Ten of these were lost in action.

A Sea Hurricane Mk IA on the catapult aboard a CAM, ready for launching, landing gear retracted and cannon orifices covered. In some cases the ships could carry several Hurricats, each machine being used once only. (Canada Archives)

rate the catapult or radio. In order to increase their effectiveness especially on long trips or through particularly dangerous zones some ships carried two or even three "Hurricats", with bases being created in their principal destination ports (Murmansk, Malta and Canada) which enabled the CAMs to "fill up" with machines before the return trip.

A first batch of fifty Sea Hurricanes Mk IAs (in fact "navalised" former RAF Mk Is) was brought out at the beginning of 1941 followed by another obtained from Canadian-made machines which were used for land-based crew training. In all nine victorious sorties were carried out by Hurricats between August 1941 and July 1943 resulting in eight kills (one double on 18 September 1942 scored over the Artic Circle by F/O Burr, from the SS Empire Morn who then managed to land his machine in Soviet territory at the end of his mission) and the death of one pilot, wounded when he bailed out.

The CAM ship Empire Lawrence with its Sea Hurricane on the prow catapult.

SPECIFICATIONS SEA HURRICANE MARK IIC

Type: Single seat fighter-bomber
Powerplant: one V-12 liquid-cooled Rolls Royce Merlin XX rated at 1 280 bhp on take off.
Dimensions
Length: 32 ft 3 in (9,84 m)
Height: 13 ft 1 in (3,99 m)
Wingspan: 40 ft (12,19 m)
Wing Surface: 257.990 sq ft (23,97 m^2)
Weight (empty): 5 867 lb (2 667 kg)
Weight (fully laden): 8 281 lb (3 674 kg)

Performances
Maximum speed: 344 mph (550 km/h)
Cruising Speed: 294 mph (470 km/h) at 20000 ft (6 100 m)
Maximum range: 463 miles (740 km) (975 miles (1 561 km) with two 44 Imp-gallon (200 l) drop tanks)
Operational Ceiling: 35 590 ft (10 850 m)
Armament
Four 20-mm cannon

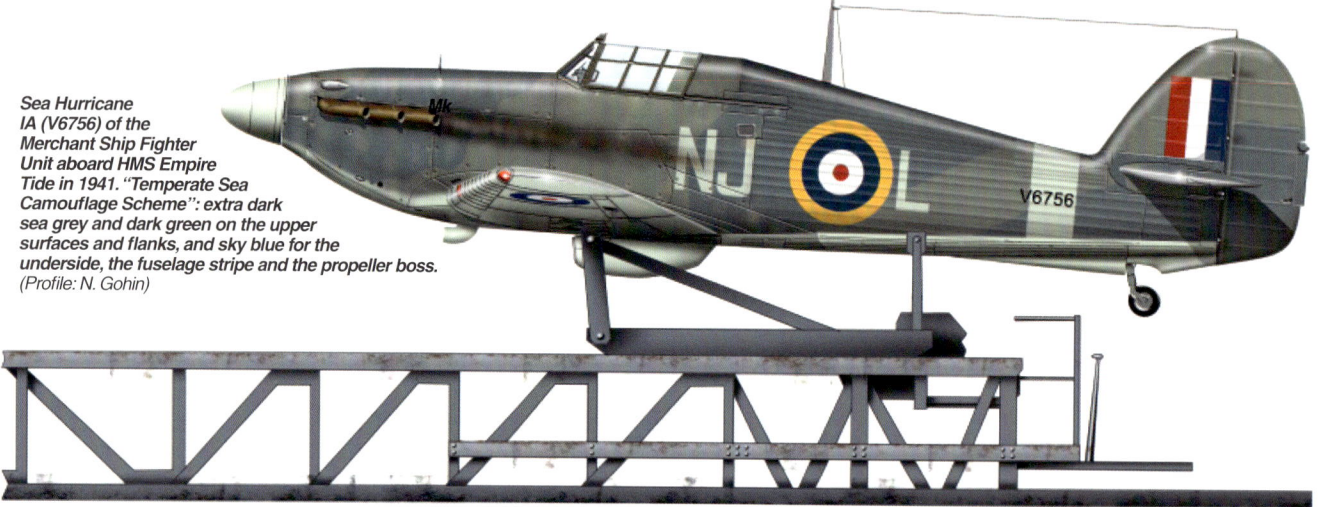

Sea Hurricane IA (V6756) of the Merchant Ship Fighter Unit aboard HMS Empire Tide in 1941. "Temperate Sea Camouflage Scheme": extra dark sea grey and dark green on the upper surfaces and flanks, and sky blue for the underside, the fuselage stripe and the propeller boss. (Profile: N. Gohin)

In August 1942 with the appearance of more escort carriers, the CAM ships sailing in the North Atlantic and the Arctic protecting the convoys coming from North America started to be withdrawn from service and the maintenance unit for the catapults based in Arkhangelsk (USSR) was disbanded the following month. The catapults on ten of the twenty-six surviving ships were removed and those CAMs still operational were sent to the Mediterranean or given the task of protecting ships on their way to Freetown (Liberia); the MSFU was officially disbanded in September 1943.

The Sea Hurricane Mk IB and Mk IC

The arrival of enough escort carriers each carrying a dozen or so machines, carriers which were in fact obtained by fitting flight decks on old merchantmen (Merchant Aircraft Carriers or MACs), gave rise to a new version of the Sea Hurricane, the Mk IB, which made up the air groups aboard.

The prototype of this version, a former Canadian Mk X (serial number P5187) was tried out in March 1941 and in the following May, converting different versions of the machines (Mk IA Sea Hurricanes that had not flown much or RAF Mk Is) started, so that in October 1941 120 Sea Hurricanes Mk IB were available. Although the archives are inaccurate and do not reveal the exact

Above.
Sea Hurricanes MK IBs being serviced below deck of an aircraft carrier. The non-folding wings limited the number of machines that could be embarked, particularly on the escort ships, which were smaller.

Opposite.
Preparing a Sea Hurricane Mk IB for a mission. Many machines were obtained by "navalising" former RAF planes like this one which has retained its exhaust dampers in front of the cockpit, a feature of night-fighters.

Above.
Catapulting a Sea Hurricane. Two rockets enabled the machine to reach a speed of 60 knots in 80 feet (25 m). The operation was commanded not by the pilot but by the CDO (Catapult Duty Officer) in charge of operating the catapult.

Opposite right.
The training of future Hurricat pilots and catapult operators was carried out by the Merchant Ship Fighter Unit (MSFU) at Speke. Here a Sea Hurricane Mk IA during land trials, painted in the "Temperate Sea Scheme".

total of converted machines, it is generally thought that between 260 and 300 differing variants and versions (Marks I, IIA or B, Canadian-built Marks X or XI or XII) were thus modified, most of them by General Aircraft Ltd.

These "Hooked Hurricanes" differed mainly by the catapult braces and their A or V-shaped arrester hooks, retracting into a housing in the rear section of the fuselage. This airframe modification was more complex than just adding the catapult braces and explains why bringing out this version took so much longer than the preceding Mk IA.

Moreover, when the landing was a little rough, a shock absorber system prevented the hook from hitting the fuselage after bouncing on the deck and a control panel light told the pilot when this hook was two-thirds out. Although trials had been carried out in 1940, the machine's fixed wings were in the end not replaced by folding ones; this would have saved space on the decks but on the other hand would have meant much more serious and involved redesigning and therefore a longer time before becoming operational.

The Sea Hurricane Mk IB, the first monoplane fighter to serve on a British aircraft-carrier, was the "navalised" variant produced in greatest numbers and therefore used most since it equipped six Fleet Air Arm squadrons; its first operational sortie took place on 7 September 1942 over the North Atlantic, an operation during which 32 enemy machines were shot down and three of the Sea Hurricanes launched by HMS Avenger lost – but all the pilots were recovered safe and sound.

The following variant, the Mark IC introduced in February 1942 was, like its land-based opposite number the Mk IIC, armed with four 20-mm cannon and equipped six FAA squadrons[6], serving mainly to intercept enemy bombers, its engine – the Merlin III rated at 1 030 bhp still in service – not really being powerful enough to confront enemy fighters effectively.

The Sea Hurricanes Mk IIC and Mk XIIA

The last British-made variant of the Sea Hurricane was the Mk IIC, obtained by modifying a land-based Mk IIC using a kit of which 70 examples were urgently bought by the Admiralty in March 1942, for the convoys sent to Malta which was daily under attack by Axis forces. Besides, it was in this theatre, during Operation Pedestal, in August 1942, that these machines flying from the aircraft-carriers HMS Eagle, Indomitable and Victorious distinguished themselves by shooting down thirty or so enemy aircraft, but at the price however of almost equivalent losses. Some months later (November 1942), the Sea Hurricane Mk IICs took part in Operation Torch, the Allied landings in North Africa which was the last time they were deployed en masse. In 1943 with the arrival of new fighter models with better performances (Seafires, Wildcat/Martlets, Hellcats and Corsairs) these planes were indeed restricted to convoy escort duties, No 385 Squadron aboard the Nairana in the Pacific, keeping its Sea Hurricane IICs until the end of the war.

The last variant of the "navalised" Hurricane was the Mark XIIA, obtained by converting fifty Canadian-made Mk XIIs and equipping them with Packard Merlin 29s rated at 1 300 bhp. Originally reserved for the RCAF, and used by them for land-based training, a certain number of examples were also supplied to the Royal Navy.

At its height, the FAA had almost 600 Sea Hurricanes of all versions and variants, of which one third were in front line units, with some planes at the end of their time even being armed with rockets after having their cannon removed.

---

6. *Nos 801, 802, 803, 880, 883 and 885.*

Opposite.
Putting an MSFU Hurricat on the catapult of a CAM Ship, Empire Tide, in 1941. In order to make taking off easier, the planes were installed on the cradle of the catapult at an angle of +5.25° which increased lift. (IWM)

Hawker Sea Hurricane Mk IB (Z4550) from No 800 Naval Air Squadron (NAS). HMS Indomitable, August 1942. With this plane, Lieutenant-Commander Bill Bruen obtained his "ace's" title on 12 August 1942 by shooting down three enemy planes (one Junkers Ju 88, one Savoia-Marchetti SM 84 and one SM 79) when his squadron was protecting a convoy heading to Malta.

Hawker Sea Hurricane Mk IB (P5206) from No 800 NAS, HMS Indomitable, August 1942. This plane bears the regulation camouflage for Sea Hurricanes (Temperate Sea Scheme) comprising dark grey (Extra Dark Sea Grey) and dark green (Dark Slate Grey) on the upper surfaces and greenish grey (Sky) on the lower surfaces. No 800 Sqn started the war with Blackburn Rocs which were replaced by Fairey Fulmars in April 1941, then by Sea Hurricanes the following year.

Hawker Sea Hurricane Mark IB (Z7153) from No 801 NAS, HMS Eagle, August 1942. During Operation Pedestal, the Sea Hurricanes were given yellow identification markings on the tail. This squadron received some Sea Hurricanes to complement the Fulmars in August 1941. Sent to the Mediterranean, first aboard HMS Argus, then Eagle, it shot down thirteen enemy machines for two Sea Hurricanes and one Fulmar.

Hawker Sea Hurricane Mk IB (AF955) from No 880 Squadron, HMS Indomitable. Madagascar, May 1942. Pilot: Lieutenant R. J. « Dickie » Cock. This squadron was given the job of intercepting and destroying Vichy aircraft during the invasion of Madagascar on 6 May 1942.

Hawker Sea Hurricane Mk I. (W9219) from No 880 NAS, Arbroath (Scotland), summer 1941. This squadron, set up in January 1941 with only three Martlets, received some Sea Hurricane Mk IIBs the following July, when it embarked aboard HMS Furious, sent to attack the town of Petsamo. On this occasion its planes were given this particular camouflage made up of dark grey (extra dark sea grey) and dark green (dark slate grey) on the upper surfaces, the under-surfaces and a large part of the fuselage being painted light grey (light grey or sky grey).

Hawker Sea Hurricane Mk IB (AF966) from No 880 NAS (Canada), HMS Indomitable. Madagascar, May 1942. When the British invaded Madagascar, the planes belonging to No 880 Sqn attacked the d'Entrecasteaux, a French aviso which ended up exploding on 6 May 1942 after going aground in the port at Diego Suarez.

Hawker Sea Hurricane Mk XII (JS310) from No 800 Squadron, HMS Biter, November 1942. The planes aboard the aircraft carrier Biter were specially given the task of knocking out French fighters during Operation Torch, the Allied landings in North Africa. On this occasion, the English roundels were replaced by American stars and the tail fin flash painted over, which made for less confusion.

Hawker Sea Hurricane Mk I (P3114). RNAS Gosport, end of 1940. This plane used earlier by No 46 Squadron, was converted to Sea Hurricane standard in November 1940; this meant that apart from having specific Royal Navy radio apparatus installed, no other navy equipment was added. Note the limit between the shades of camouflage, situated very high up on the fuselage.

Hawker Sea Hurricane Mk IIC (NF728) from No 760 Squadron, HMS Ravager, October 1944. This unit, attached to the Royal Navy Fighter School, was at the time training pilots for anti-submarine warfare.

Hawker Sea Hurricane Mk IIC (NF668) from No 825 Squadron, HMS Vindex, March 1944. This squadron was given the task of protecting the North Atlantic convoys from submarine attack at the beginning of 1944, and this plane was one of five Sea Hurricanes officially chosen to test the use of rockets at sea.

Hawker Sea Hurricane Mk IB (V7506) from No 885 Squadron, HMS Victorious, October 1942. This aircraft carrier which carried six Hurricanes as interceptors, took part with HMS Eagle, Indomitable and Furious in Operation Pedestal, supplying Malta under siege by Axis forces ending on 15 August 1942, when the last boat reached the Grand Harbour.

Hawker Sea Hurricane Mk I (Z4867) from Merchant Ship Fighter Unit, Speke, end of 1941. The MSFU was given the task of training pilots for operating Sea Hurricanes aboard CAM ships (Catapult Aircraft Merchant ships), the ships which were equipped with a catapult for protecting convoys from air attack.

Above.
A line up of Hurricane Mk Is of the 2/I/2 "Chardons Blancs" of the Belgian Air Force in 1940. Most of these planes were destroyed on the ground in the early hours of the German attack in May the same year. (SHD Air)

THE FOREIGN USERS OF THE HURRICANE

Belgium

Because getting the locally-built Renard 36 fighter into service had been delayed, Belgium decided in the meantime to buy some Hurricanes off England which in March 1939 agreed to hand over twenty Mk Is intended originally for the RAF. Fifteen of those fighters were indeed delivered before the war (the first in May and the last in September) with the five remaining examples being kept in England after the beginning of hostilities. Meanwhile in June 1939, a contract for the production under licence of eighty Mk Is by Fairey, at Gosselies and SABCA (SA Belge de Construction d'Avions) was signed with Hawker, these planes equipped with engines supplied by Great Britain differing only in their armament which comprised four 12.65-mm machine guns instead of the original eight 7.7-mm guns.

While four RAF machines had been interned by Belgium, officially a neutral country during the Phoney War and incorporated into the Aéronautique Militaire, the first Belgian-made Hurricane was delivered in April 1940, while two others were undergoing trials when the Germans attacked in May 1940.

At that moment the country had twelve machines assigned to the 2nd Escadrille of the 1st Group of the 2nd Régiment d'Aéronautique (2/I/2 "Chardons" – thistles) stationed at Diest-Schaffen. None of them were destroyed on the ground during the first hours of the attack, the survivors managing to escape to Beauchevain where they were then destroyed the next day during an air raid.

At the end of the war, three Mk IICs were used for liaison (carrying mail quickly from England to Belgium) by the Metropolitan Communication Squadron 367, which became the 21st Escadrille of the Belgian Air Force after the war. These planes were handed over to the advanced pilot training school and withdrawn from service a few months later.

Canada

Canada itself used a lot of licence-built Hurricanes to defend its territory (in Nos 125, 126, 127, 129 and 130 Squadrons RCAF) and for training its pilots or the RAF's, especially those taking part in the Empire Training Scheme, a common training programme set up by the two countries.

Egypt

The Royal Egyptian Air Force (REAF) received its first Hurricanes in July 1942 and put them into service with its No 17 Squadron, but because of maintenance problems these planes remained non-operational for most of 1943. Egypt was officially neutral but offered to protect the East Mediterranean sea routes so Great Britain supplied it with what it needed to re-equip its original squadron with new planes. Eighteen Mk IICs were therefore delivered between September 1943 and February 1944 with the aircraft carrying out their first operational mission – convoy escort – on 26 March 1944. No17 Squadron, re-designated No2 in April of the same year, was at first placed under British command, attached to No 219 Group; it then came under Egyptian command in February of the following year. No 2 Squadron REAF's Hurricanes were replaced by Spitfires and the surviving machines transferred for a while to No 6 Squadron.

Eire

The first three Hurricanes of the Irish Army Air Corps were in reality three RAF planes interned at the beginning of the war following a forced landing on Irish soil. After protracted negotiations, two of them were sub-

Opposite.
The Irish Army Air Corps owned a total of about fifteen Hurricanes of various types which were all assigned to No 1 Squadron and used until 1947. In the foreground is a Mark I received in February 1944.

sequently swapped for Mk Is from the initial production series. A fourth machine was delivered in July 1943, followed in 1944 by seven Mk Is, then by six Mk IICs in March 1945. In 1945 the IAAC had fifteen or so Hurricanes all assigned to No 1 Squadron based at Baldonnel remaining in service until 1947.

Finland

Twelve Mk Is bought in a roundabout way after the beginning of the Winter War were delivered via Sweden by air but in the end they weren't used before the Armistice in March 1940. Used first by Lentolaivue 22, then 28, in May 1940 then by the HeLLv 30 at the end of August, some of them were fitted with skis instead of wheels (including the tail-wheel). Registered as HC-451 to 460, the Finnish Hurricanes took an active part in the fighting against the USSR during the Continuation War beginning on 25 June 1941, alongside a captured Russian machine also being used by the Ilmavoimat. Withdrawn from service in May 1944, some examples were assigned to defending the capital, Helsinki. The Hurricanes were the best fighters Finland had until the arrival of German Bf 109Gs and were used mainly for interception because of their short range.

France

After the Syrian Campaign, the Groupe de Chasse No 1 "Alsace" of the FAFL (Forces Aériennes Françaises Libres – Free French Air Force) was formed and equipped with Morane Saulnier MS 406s before it received Hurricane Mk Is when it settled at Ismalaya (Egypt) in January 1942. After they had acquitted themselves remarkably well against the better equipped and more numerous Germans, the Alsace pilots, who had scored two kills (including one by Aspirant Mailfert who cut off the tail of a Bf 109F with his wing) during the retreat in June 1942, replaced their wheezy old machines with some Mk IIs when they settled in Alexandria. They did not have the opportunity to use them a lot since the Alsace left the Middle East the following September for England to become No 341 Squadron RAF.

Other units in the newly re-created Armée de l'Air in North Africa used Hurricanes, like GC 2/3 "Dauphiné", which exchanged its old Dewoitine D.520s for some Mk IICs at the end of October 1943, which were in turn replaced by P-47Ds in April 1944; or GC2/3 "Ardennes", one of whose squadrons used Hurricanes to protect the coast of Palestine before exchanging them for P-39s.

Some Mk IICs also served in the Ecole de Chasse at Meknès in 1945-1946, while a dozen Sea Hurricane Mk IICs and Mk XIIs, recovered in rather murky circumstances in North Africa and equipped with tropical filters were used by the Aéronavale until 1946.

Persia

18 Hurricane Mk Is were ordered by Persia (present-day Iran) in August 1939 but only two of them were in fact delivered in the first months of the Second World War, the delay being due to difficulties in making the dust filters. Ten Mk IICs arrived in the country in 1943, the rest of the order being supplied after the war, i.e. sixteen further Mk IIcs and two two-seaters. All these were used at the training school at Doshan Teppeh, the two-seaters being fitted with Tempest-style rear cockpit canopies in order to avoid turbulence at that very spot when the planes went above 280 mph (450 kph).

A shot of one of the Yugoslav Air Force Hurricanes banking, showing its aluminium underside and its roundels surmounted by the "Cross of Kosovo", an emblem retained until 1941. The country built this fighter under licence but they were all destroyed when the country was invaded by the Axis forces in April 1941.

Above and opposite.
The Fighter Group (Groupe de Chasse No 1) "Alsace" of the FAFL equipped with MS 406s to start with, received its Hurricane Mk Is when it settled in Egypt in January 1942. These former RAF machines were repainted in the colours of their new owners, especially the Croix de Lorraine on the fuselage and occasionally a tricolour propeller boss. The machine nick-named "Theodore" belonged to Commandant Joseph Pouliquen, then boss of the "Alsace", who created GC 3 "Normandie", the future "Normandie-Niemen", in 1943. (SHD Air).

Poland

A single example (L2048) was delivered to Poland on 8 August 1939 before the country was invaded by the Germans; the nine others to be delivered were deviated to Gibraltar which they never reached because the ship carrying them was sunk (it is worth mentioning that some sources say that Great Britain never actually sent these planes in the first place!).

Portugal

Portugal which was neutral during WWII, obtained the delivery of several dozen Hurricanes from Britain at the end of the war in exchange for using its bases in the Azores during the war. Fifty end-of-production tropicalised Mk IICs were returned to Hawker's Langley factory where they were re-fitted with Merlin 22s and had their tropical filters removed. Forty serviceable planes were convoyed to Portugal together with a large batch of spare parts. These planes were assigned to Base No 3 at Tancos and to the Lisbon defence squadron, and remained in service until 1951 when some of them returned to England to take part in the shooting of the film "Angel One Five".

Rumania

Rumania ordered fifty Hurricanes of which twelve had been delivered by the outbreak of the war, but deliveries ceased when the country decided to join the Axis powers. Opinion is considerably divided as to how the Rumanians used their Hurricanes. Some sources state that these

Below.
Persia was the only country to receive Hurricane two-seaters, after the war; the rear cockpit was equipped with a similar canopy to the Tempest's.

Hurricane Mk II of the Türk Hava Kuvetleri, the Turkish Air Force, which received in all 26 machines between 1939 and 1942; Great Britain with this supply of arms, hoped to keep the country from joining the Axis forces. (THK)

machines were assigned to the 55th Fighter Squadron with the task of defending the port at Constanza and that they shot down several Russian I-16s at the beginning of Operation Barbarossa, and that the future ace Cantacuzino scored his first kills aboard this type. Other sources state on the contrary that these machines were never in front line use and were only used in the service role, with a lack of spare parts leading to their being replaced at the beginning of 1943 by IAR-80s.

Turkey

Twelve Hurricane MkIs were delivered to Turkey in September-October 1939 followed by fourteen Mk IIBs and IICs in 1942, deliveries being made by Great Britain including among others Spitfires, Beauforts and Beaufighters taken from RAF stocks, so that this neutral country would not join the Axis powers in the conflict.

USSR

The first Hurricanes to serve on Soviet soil were those in No 151 Wing RAF, which included Nos 81 and 134 Squadrons which were based at Vaenga near Murmansk, in September 1941. Shipped there by the aircraft carrier Argus, these Mk IIBs carried out escort missions for Soviet bombers and convoy protection to Murmansk, Petsamo and Arkangelsk. After training pilots and ground personnel on the Hurricane, the British left Vaenga on 28 November 1941 and handed over the thirty-nine remaining serviceable Hurricanes to the 72nd Air Regiment of the Soviet Navy.

About 3 000 Hurricanes (the exact figure is not known – it varies from 2270 to 2952) were also supplied to the Soviet Union almost until the end of the war. These were mainly Mk IIBs and IICs (80% of the total) but also a few Mk IIDs and Mk IVs (perhaps thirty or so) – machines produced in Canada and sent straight to the USSR by sea. Quite a large number were lost during shipment, the ships carrying them being sunk by the Germans. Most Russian Hurricanes served near where they landed, i.e. on the Northern Front, in the Air Force and in the Navy Air Force.

Yugoslavia

Yugoslavia was the first foreign country to purchase a Hurricane, in 1938 with an order for a further twelve Mk Is with fabric-covered wings. The first plane delivered flew for the first time on 15 December 1938 and a second batch of twelve planes, with metal wings and powered this time by a Merlin II driving a three-blade propeller, was then delivered at the beginning of 1940.

Apart from the aircraft built in Great Britain, the Rogozarski Company in Belgrade had been allowed to build forty machines under licence, whilst the Fabrika Aeroplana Hidroplana at Zmaj was to have done likewise for a further sixty. A dozen planes had been indeed built when the country was invaded on 6 April 1941, which meant that 38 Hurricanes were operational with the 51st Fighter Squadron (2nd Regiment) at Sarajevo and in the 33rd and 34th Squadrons (4th Regiment) based at Zagreb. The Yugoslav army fought for eight days before withdrawing to Greece which only one or two planes were able to rally, most of those still airworthy were grounded because of the thick fog which covered their bases, and destroyed on 14 April to prevent them from falling into enemy hands.

Opposite left.
General Kuznetzov, commanding the North Sea Fleet, aboard Mk IIB V5252/01, the first Hurricane piloted by a Russian. This former RAF plane from NO151 Wing had been brought to Vaenga on the aircraft carrier HMS Argus.

Hurricane MkI (H-27) from the 2/1/2 (2nd Escadrille of the 1st Groupe of the 2nd Regiment "les Chardons Blancs", Belgian Air Force, Diest, Belgium, May 1940. At the time the Germans attacked, Belgium had 11 Hurricanes at its disposal, almost all destroyed in the air raids in the first hours of the conflict.

Hurricane Mk I (V6613) from No 1 Fighter Squadron of the Irish Army Air Corps, Baldonnel, Eire, 1945. This plane, a former No 111 Squadron RAF plane was delivered to Eire in July 1943. In all Eire had fifteen or so Hurricanes which were all assigned to No 1 Squadron, remaining in service until 1947.

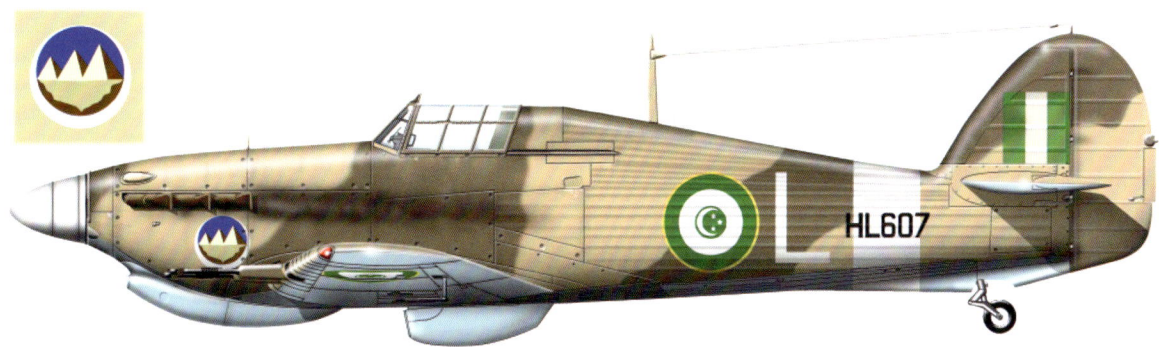

Hurricane Mk IIC (HL607) from No 2 Squadron, Royal Egyptian Air Force, Marsa Matruh, Egypt, 1944. The REAF's No 17 Squadron was re-designated No 2 Squadron in April 1944 and was at first placed under British command, then came under Egyptian officers the following February. When the Hurricanes were replaced by Spitfires, the surviving machines were transferred for a while to No 6 Squadron.

Hurricane Mk I (HC451) of the Lentolaivue 32 (LLv 32 – 32nd Squadron) of the Suomen Ilmavoimat (Finnish Air Force), Immola, Finland, 1941. Finland bought 12 Hurricane Mk 1s at the beginning of 1940 which were convoyed there by air in March, one of them being damaged during the transfer. Arriving there too late for the Winter War, the eight surviving machines, assigned to LeLv 32 then later to LeLv 10 under the name "Osasto (Detachment) Kalaja" took part in the Continuation War in 1941 during which they scored five and a half kills.

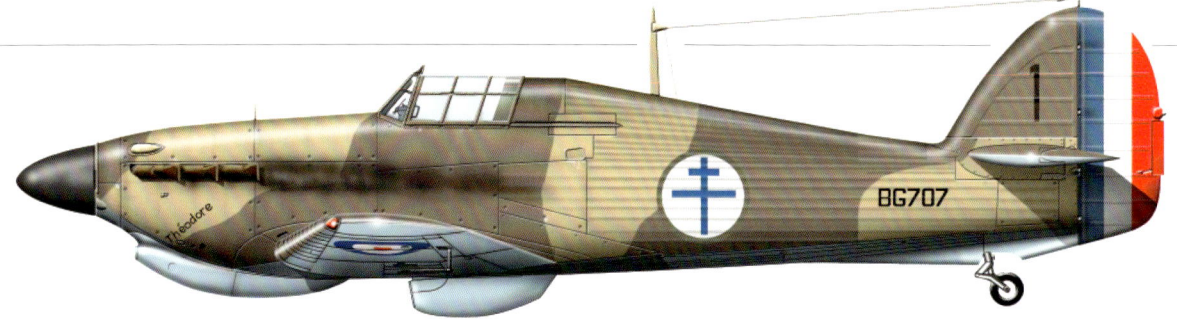

Hurricane Mk I (BG707) from Groupe de Chasse No 1 (GC 1) "Alsace" of the Forces Aériennes Françaises Libres (FAFL), Amriyah (Suez Canal Zone), Egypt, September 1942. "Théodore", a former No 111 Squadron RAF machine was the plane usually flown by Commandant Pouliquen.

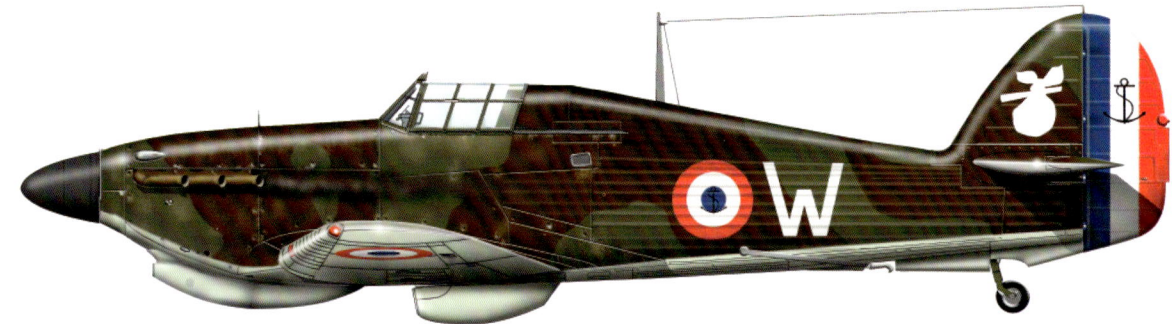

Hurricane Mk XII (Serial number unknown) from the French Aéronavale. Fifteen or so Sea Hurricane Mk IICs and XIIs, including this machine which took part in the 14 July 1945 parade, equipped with tropical filters, were recovered in rather murky circumstances in North Africa and used by the Aéronavale until 1946.

Hurricane Mk II (BE225) from 2-VLG-IV (2 Jachtafdelingen – 2nd Fighter Flight – of the IV Vliegtuiggrorp – Fighter group), of the *Militaire Luchtvaart van het Koninklijk Nederlands Indisch Leger* (ML-KNIL) Royal Dutch East Indies, Kalidjati, Java, beginning of 1942. The ML-KNIL ordered 12 Mk Is in 1941 which were never delivered for lack of engines. On the other hand, 24 IIBs destined originally for RAF units in Singapore were sent to the Dutch East Indies when the town fell. These fighters which retained their camouflage equipped two flights and fought the Japanese invaders in February and March 1942.

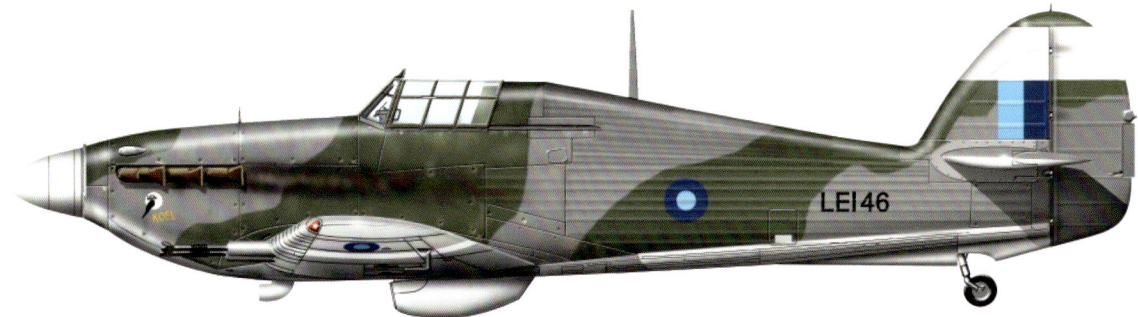

Hurricane Mk IIC (LE146) from No 2 Squadron of the Royal Indian Air Force, Akyab, Burma, 1945. The RIAF received several Mk Is for training, a first unit (No 1 Squadron) being formed with Mk IIBs at the end of the same year. In 1943, about 200 Mk IIBs and Cs taken from English stocks were delivered from which seven squadrons were formed and fought in Burma. A lot of Hurricanes were still in service at the time India won its independence in 1947.

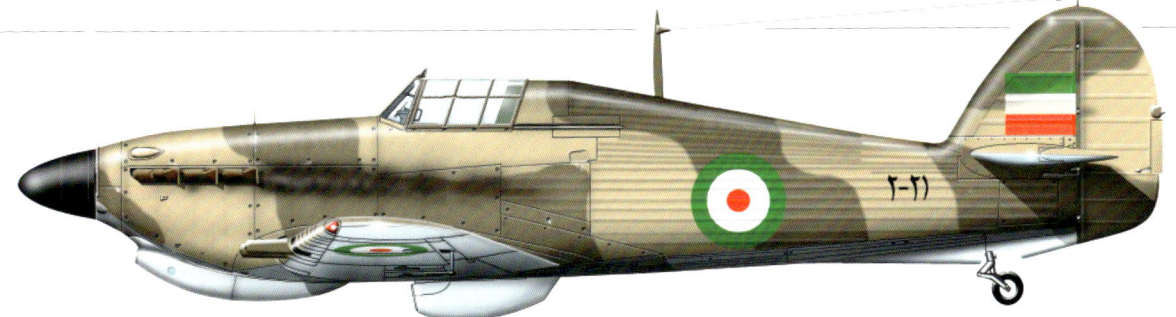

Hurricane Mk IIC (2-21) from the Persian Air Force Flying School, Doshan Teppeh, Iran, 1947. Two of the eighteen Hurricane Mk Is ordered by Persia (present-day Iran) in 1939 were indeed delivered and were joined by ten Mk IICs in 1943 and finally by sixteen other Mk IICs, and 2 two-seaters after the war. All were used for training at the flying school at Doshan Teppeh.

Hurricane Mk IIC (591) from *Escadrilha "RV"* of the *Aeronautica Militar Portuguesa, Espinho, Portugal*, 1947. Portugal received forty or so restored Hurricane Mk IICs after the Second World War and kept them until 1951; some of them were returned to England where they took part in the shooting of several films.

Hurricane Mk I from the *Escadrila 53 Vanatoare* (53rd Fighter Squadron) of the Fortele Aeriene Regale Ale Romaniei (Romanian Air Force), Constanza, Romania, June 1941. Aboard this plane, the one usually flown by Captain Emila Georgescu, the pilot Hiria Agarici shot down a Soviet SB bomber on 23 June 1941. The Romanian planes kept their original British camouflage scheme; only the yellow identification marks were added on the fuselage and the wings.

Hurricane Mk IIB (BN233) from the 78. IAP- SF (Istrebitel'niy Aviapolk - air regiment of the Syevernoe Flota – North Sea Fleet), Vaenga, USSR, beginning of 1942. This regiment, commanded by this plane's pilot, Major Boris Feoklistovich Safonov, was formed when the machines of No 151 Wing RAF were transferred to the VVS (Voyenno Vozdushne Sily – Soviet Air Force). Safonov, an ace with twenty kills to his credit and twice Hero of the Soviet Union was shot down in aerial combat on 31 May 1942.

Hurricane Mk IIB (Serial number unknown) from the 78. IAP-SF, Vaenga, USSR, beginning of 1942. The pilot of this plane, Captain Vassili Semyonovitch Adokin, showed his successes in the shape of stars painted on the fuselage: those edged with white were his own; those without the group's. The Hurricanes used by the Soviet units retained their original markings and camouflage, as here with the regulation RAF sky blue fuselage stripe.

Hurricane Mk IID (KX248) from the 246. IAP, 1944. Out of more than 3 000 Hurricanes received by the USSR only 46 were Mk IIDs equipped with 20-mm cannon housed in underwing gondolas.

Hurricane Mk IID (KX248) from the 246. IAP, Stalingrad Region, 1943. All the Mk IIDs supplied to the USSR were assigned to the 246 IAP and used until they were replaced by Yak-1s in the summer of 1944.

Hurricane Mk IIB (BM959) from the 609. IAP, Murmansk, USSR, end of 1942. This plane, piloted by Sub-Lieutenant Ivan Babanin, made a forced landing in Finland on 6 April 1942. The fuselage inscription reads "Long live Stalin" (with "For the Motherland" on the right-hand side). This regiment was given the task of protecting this large White Sea port and was also equipped with LaGG-3s.

Hurricane Mk IIB (serial number unknown) from the 22. ZAP (Zapasnnoy Aviatsionnyi Polk – reserve air regiment), Ivanovo, USSR, 1942. There is some doubt as to this plane's exact colour scheme; it could be the "desert" scheme. As a general rule machines equipped with tropical filters were delivered to the USSR from the Middle East, the others were delivered by sea via Murmansk.

Hurricane Mk IIA (Z2889) from an unidentified fighter regiment attached to the 6. PVO (Protivovozdushnaya Oborona - air defence), Moscow Region, USSR, 1942. This plane from a former RAF night fighter unit (No 238 and 242 Squadrons) retained its original black (Special Night) camouflage; only the new owners' markings were added.

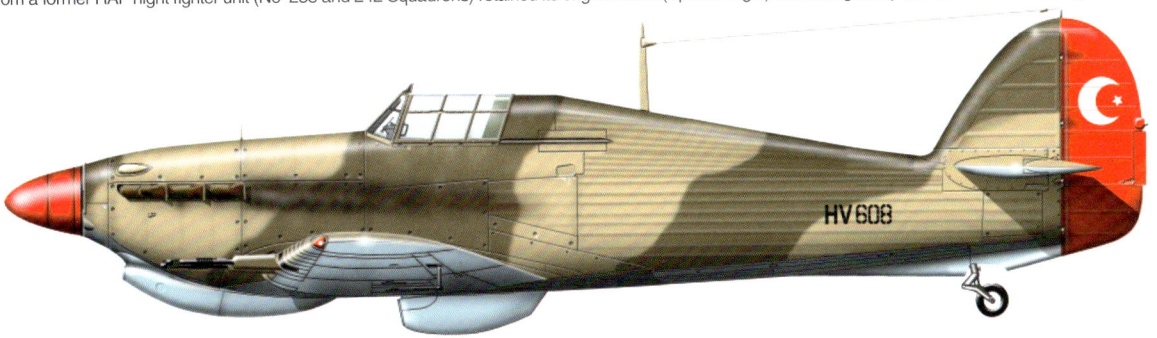

Hurricane Mk IIC (HV608) from the Türk Hava Kuvvetleri (Turkish Air force), 1942. Twelve Hurricane Mk Is were delivered to Turkey in 1939 followed by fourteen Mk IIBs and IICs in 1942, these deliveries being made by Great Britain to prevent this country from joining the Axis forces during the conflict.

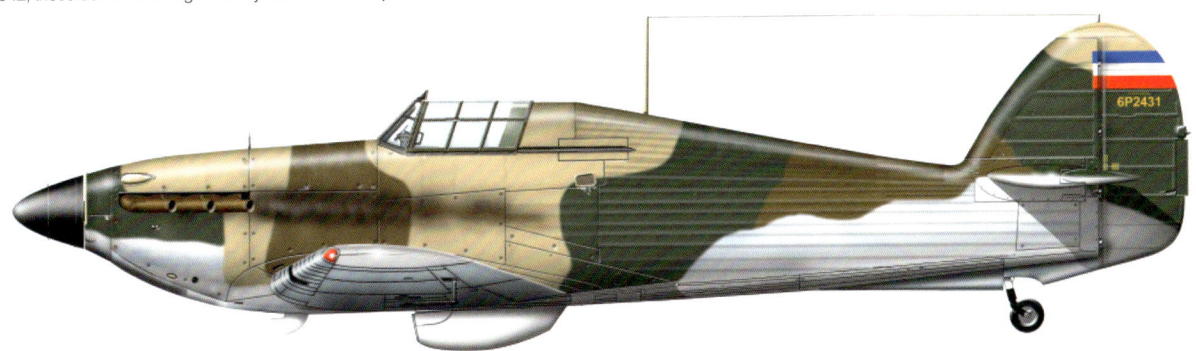

Hurricane Mk I (2341) from the Jugoslovensko Kraljevsko Ratno Vazduhoplovsto (JKRV – Royal Yugoslav Air Force). Apart from the 24 Mk Is bought before the war, Yugoslavia built fifteen or so other examples under licence. At the time of the German attack in 1941, thirty or so were operational but were all destroyed within a week. The Yugoslav Hurricanes bore various camouflage schemes including this one, with three colours (dark green, beige and brown) on the upper surfaces and aluminium lower surfaces, without any roundels, like the flanks on the fuselage of this example.

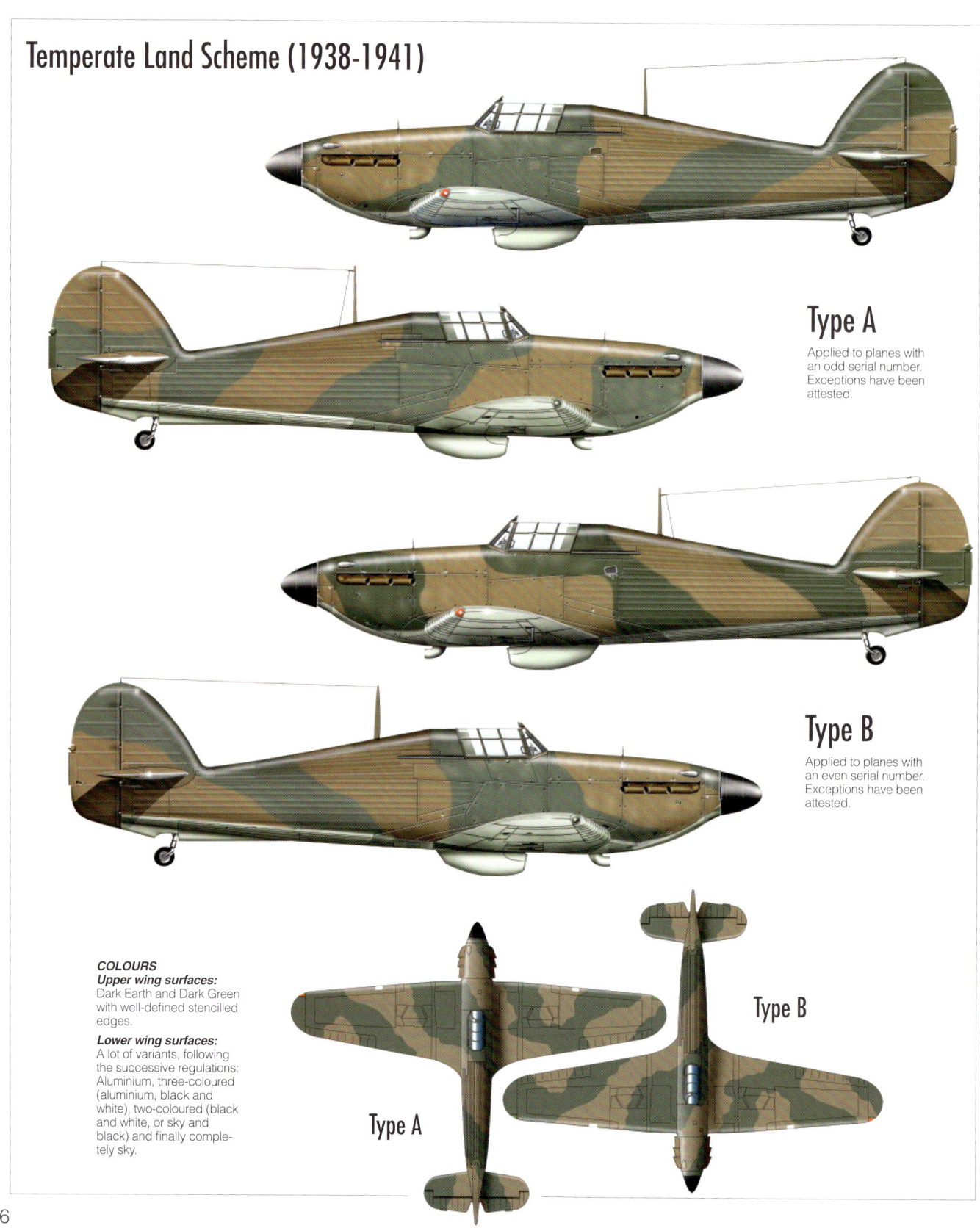

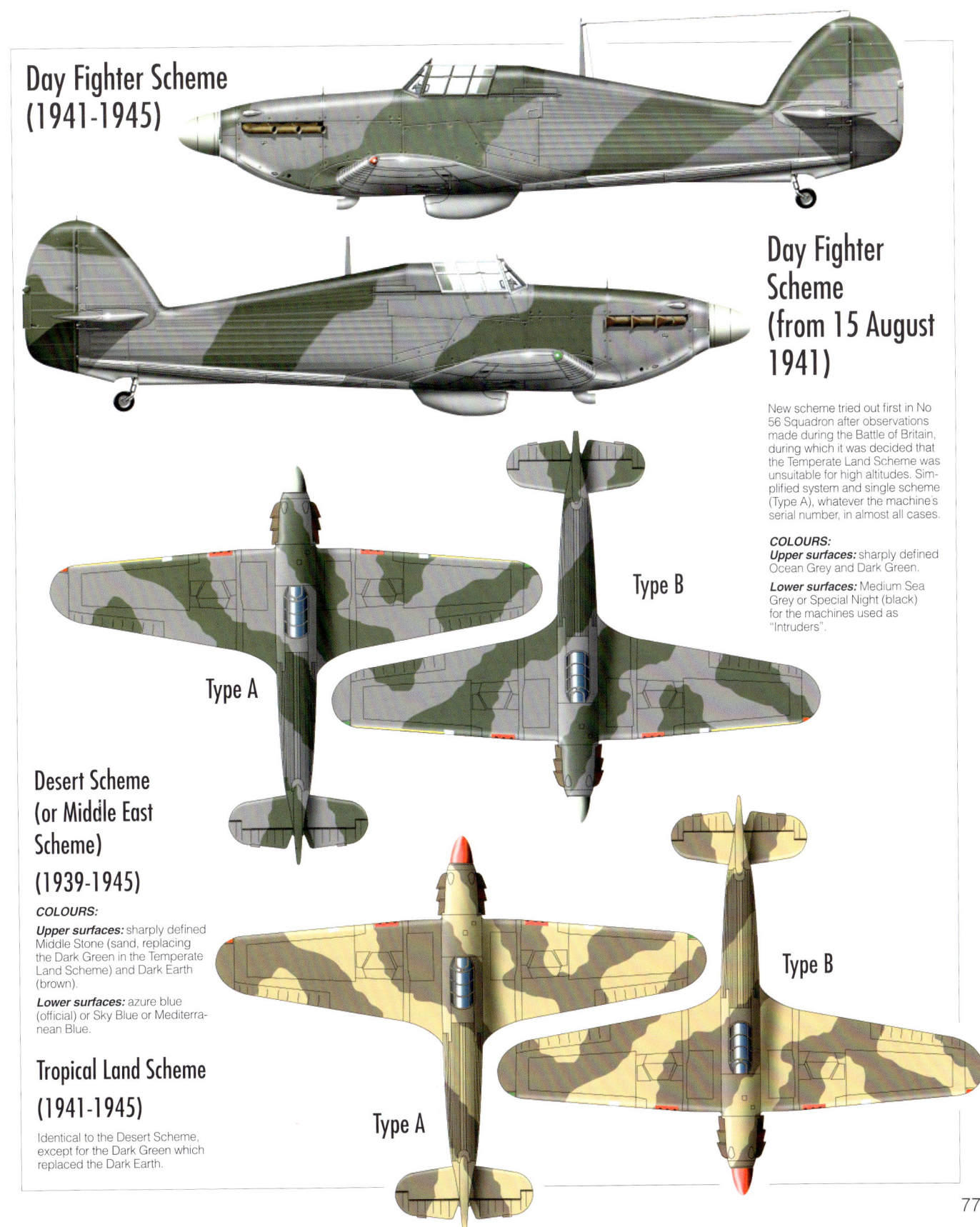

Under surfaces camouflage schemes

— Original series model, entirely aluminium. Type A 45" (114.30 cm) roundels placed 57" (144.78 cm) from the wing tip. Serial number repeated on each wing, in reverse order and in big characters (30"/76.20 cm).

— The first two-colour model (black on the left, white on the right), identical to the previous model but with the outer part of the wing black (on the left) and white (on the right). The serial number is painted in sharp contrast to the background colour.

— Scheme introduced during the Munich Crisis in September 1938. Left wing black and right white. The rest of the underside, including ailerons and flaps, was aluminium. No roundels.

— Scheme used by Hurricanes deployed in France (Nos 60 and 67 Wings) with roundels (Type A) added following the 2 September 1939 directive.

— Three-coloured production series scheme: aluminium fuselage and wings divided in two equal halves.

— Two-coloured scheme with the colours merging mid-fuselage. The roundels were added according to an official directive dated 15 May 1940 but did not last long since they disappeared when the Sky colour was introduced for the lower surfaces two weeks later.

— The "Sky" colour (a light greenish grey) was introduced officially on 6 June 1940. Before the regulation shade was supplied to the fighting units or applied directly at the factory, several substitute shades were used, among which were mainly "Duck Egg Blue" also called Sky Blue (a colour tending towards blue), "Air Ministry Pale Blue" (pale blue) and the poetic "Eau de Nil" (greener than the standard Sky) also called "Duck Egg Green".

— The underwing roundels were reintroduced after 1 August 1940. The diameter varied, with the 45 inches (114,30 cm) roundel being the most common.

— The black left wing was also reintroduced on 27 November 1940 at the same time as the fuselage stripe and the propeller spinner, both usually painted light blue (Sky Blue).

— Overall black colour scheme (Special Night) introduced from 22 May 1940 onwards for planes operating at night (fighters or intruders). Roundels on the lower surfaces were not compulsory.
Special Night was officially replaced by "Smooth Night Finish", a satin finish black colour, in October 1942.

New Day Fighter Scheme introduced on 15 August 1941. Medium Sea Grey underside, yellow identification stripes on the outer part of the leading edges, usually 45 in-diameter Type A roundels.

— A new type of roundel (Type C) was introduced in May 1942. Placed 80 in (203.20 cm) from the wing tip, it was a regulation 32 in (81.28 cm) in diameter. This configuration was retained until the end of the war.

The Different types of roundels

Type A

25 Inches (63,50 cm) | 35 Inches (88,90 cm) | 35 Inches (88,90 cm) | 45 Inches (114,30 cm) | 35 Inches (88,90 cm) | 49 Inches (124,46 cm)

Type B

15 Inches (38,10 cm) | 25 Inches (63,5 cm) | 35 Inches (88,9 cm) | 49 Inches (124,46 cm)

Type C

32 Inches (81,28 cm) | 36 Inches (91,44 cm) | SEAC 18 Inches (45,72 cm)

The Different Hurricane Versions

Prototype (K5083)

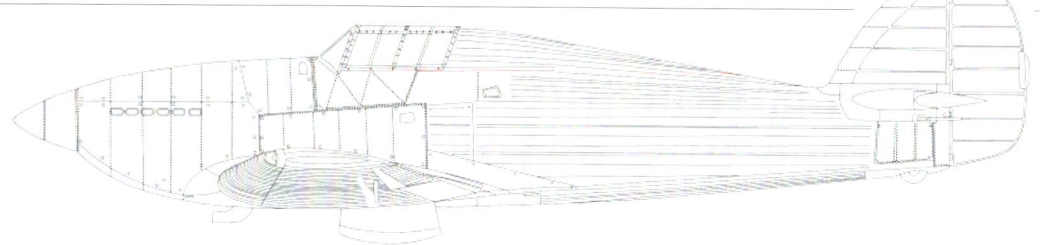

990 bhp Rolls Royce Merlin C engine. Two-blade wooden fixed pitch Watts airscrew. Fabric covered wings, retractable tailwheel, and tailplane with struts.

Mark I

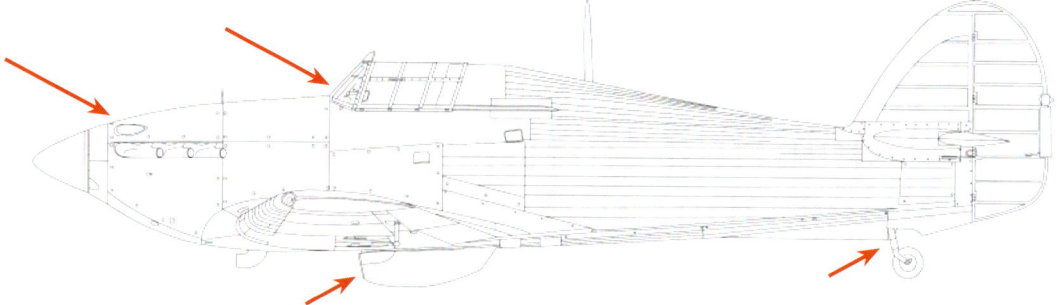

Remodelled canopy, fixed tailwheel with under-fuselage "keel" added after the 61st production series example. Rolls Royce Merlin II or III rated at 1 030 bhp. First examples with fabric-covered wings and wooden two-blade Watts propeller, then metal wings and three-bladed propeller, the de Havilland Hydromatic to begin with, then the Rotol constant speed airscrew. Armed with four .303 (7.7 mm) Browning machine guns in the each wing leading edge. Final examples produced with reinforced protection (extra armour).

Mark IIB Trop

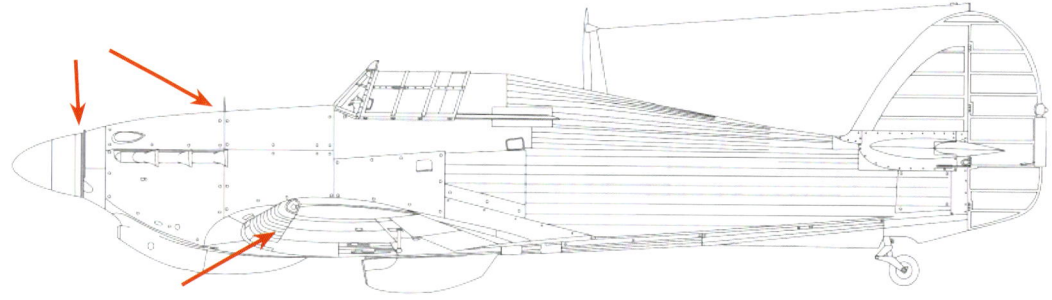

Identical to the Mk I from the end of production, but the fuselage was 4 1/3 inches longer (a extra section was added just in front of the cockpit), with new two-stage supercharged Merlin XX rated at 1 185 bhp.
— Mk IIA: armament consisting of eight .303 machine guns. Some examples obtained by converting Mk Is.
— Mk IIB (originally designated "Mk IIA Series 2"): ditto, but armament increased to twelve .303 Browning machine guns; so-called "Universal Wing" with two extra underwing attachment points taking up to 1 000 lb of bombs or drop tanks, etc.
— Mk IIB Trop: "tropicalised" version of previous machine with Vokes or Rolls Royce dust filter added in a fairing under the nose, in front of the carburettor air intake; and survival kit.
Identical to the end of production Mk Is but fuselage lengthened by some 4 1/3 inches (extra section added in front of the cockpit) and new two-stage supercharged Merlin XX rated at 1 185 bhp.

Mark IIC

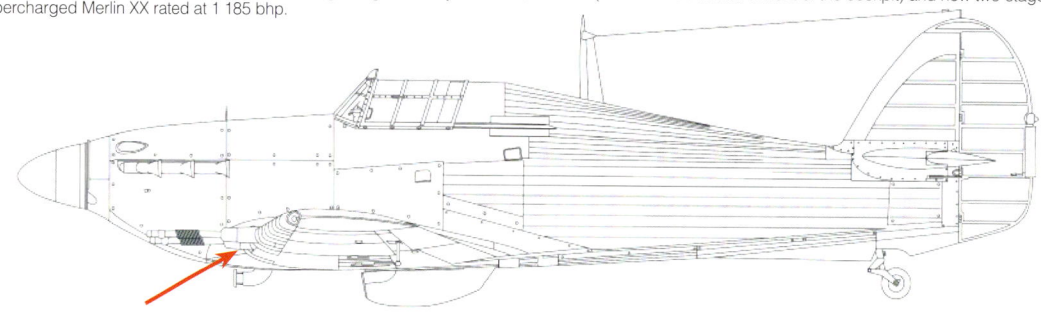

— Mark IIC: armament comprising four 20-mm cannon mounted in pairs in the wings. Attachment points for external loads (drop tanks or bombs).
— Mk IID: armament consisting of two 40-mm Vickers cannon. Two wing-mounted machine guns were retained to improve aiming. Most of the examples were tropicalised with dust filters added in a fairing under the nose.

Mark IV

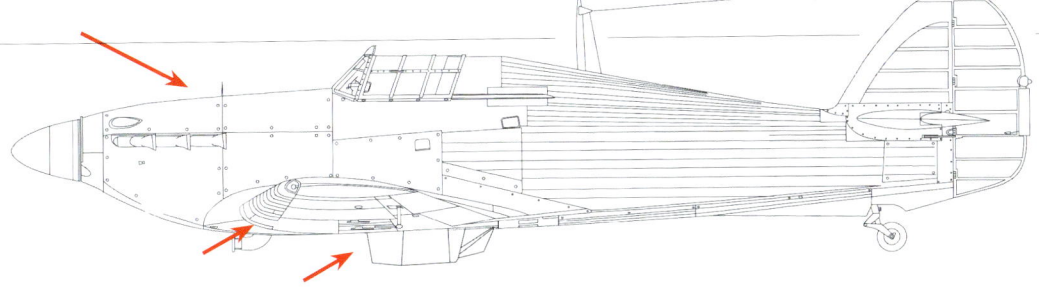

Initially designated "Mark IIE". Rolls Royce Merlin 24 or 27 rated at 1 280 bhp. "Universal" wing with two .303 Browning machine guns; could be equipped with rockets, drop tanks, bombs or cannon in underwing gondolas. A lot were tropicalised.

Sea Hurricane

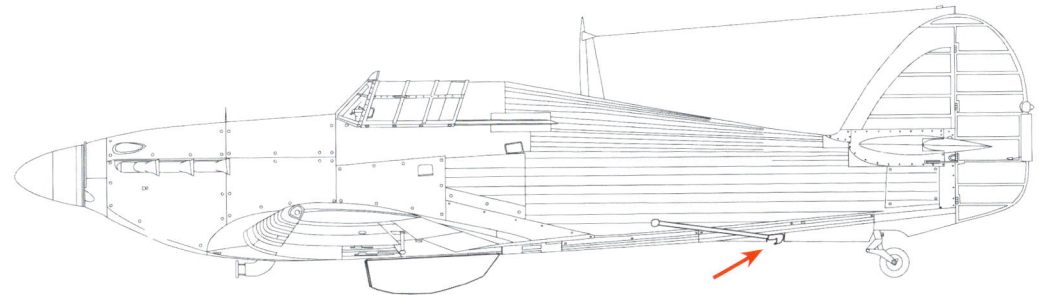

— **Sea Hurricane Mk IA:** version intended to equip the escort ships fitted with a catapult (CAM ships). Identical to the standard Mk I but with specific Royal Navy equipment fitted, reinforced fuselage, extra stowage rings and catapult hooks.
— **Sea Hurricane Mk IB:** identical to the land version but with catapult braces and two-pronged arrester hook (the so-called "A" or "V" hooks), retracting into the rear of the fuselage.
— **Sea Hurricane Mark IC:** identical to the Mk IIC with four 20-mm cannon, catapult braces and arrester hook.
-- **Sea Hurricane Mark IIC:** identical to the Mk IIC, obtained by converting "land" versions.
— **Sea Hurricane Mark XIIA:** navalised version of the MK XII made in Canada and powered by a Packard Merlin 29 rated at 1 300 bhp.

Hurricane squadron codes

Royal Air Force

Code	Squadron
AD	113 Sqn
AE	402 Sqn
AK	213 Sqn
AL	79 Sqn
AP	186 Sqn
AV	121 Sqn
AW	42 Sqn
BQ	451 Sqn
BR	184 Sqn
DT	257 Sqn
DU	312 Sqn
DX	245 Sqn
DZ	151 Sqn
EF	232 Sqn
EL	181 Sqn
EY	80 Sqn
F3	438 Sqn
FG	335 Sqn
FJ	261 Sqn/164 Sqn
FM	257 Sqn
FN	331 Sqn
FT	43 Sqn
FV	81 Sqn
GG	151 Sqn
GN	249 Sqn
GO	94 Sqn
GQ	134 Sqn
GV	134 Sqn
GZ	32 Sqn
HA	261 Sqn
HB	229 Sqn/239 Sqn
HE	263 Sqn
HF	183 Sqn
HH	260 Sqn
HV	73 Sqn
I4	567 Sqn
I8	440 Sqn
II	116 Sqn
JH	317 Sqn
JT	256 Sqn
JU	111 Sqn
JV	6 Sqn
JX	1 Sqn
KC	238 Sqn
KT	32 Sqn
KW	615 Sqn
KZ	287 Sqn
LD	250 Sqn
LE	242 Sqn
LK	87 Sqn
LR	56 Sqn/146 Sqn
M4	587 Sqn
MF	5260 Sqn
ML	605 Sqn
MR	245 Sqn
MS	273 Sqn
MU	60 Sqn
NA	1 Sqn
NN	310 Sqn
NO	85 Sqn
NQ	43 Sqn
NV	79 Sqn
NW	33 Sqn/286 Sqn
OK	450 Sqn
OP	3 Sqn
PD	87 Sqn/450 Sqn
PO	46 Sqn
QO	3 Sqn
RE	229 Sqn
RF	303 Sqn
RG	208 Sqn
RJ	46 Sqn
RP	288 Sqn
RS	33 Sqn/30 Sqn
SA	486 Sqn
SD	501 Sqn
SF	137 Sqn
SO	145 Sqn
SV	439 Sqn
SW	253 Sqn
SZ	316 Sqn
TM	111 Sqn/504 Sqn
TP	73 Sqn
UF	601 Sqn
US	56 Sqn
UV	17 Sqn
UZ	306 Sqn
VK	238 Sqn
VY	85 Sqn
WC	309 Sqn
WG	128 Sqn
WN	527 Sqn
XE	123 Sqn
XM	182 Sqn
XP	174 Sqn
XR	71 Sqn
YB	17 Sqn
YE	239 Sqn
YK	80 Sqn
YO	401 Sqn
ZH	401 Sqn
ZY	247 Sqn
3M	679 Sqn
4M	695 Sqn
5O	521 Sqn
6D	20/631 Sqn
8Q	34 Sqn

Royal Navy (Fleet Air Arm)

Code	Squadron
K1	766 Sqn
M2	768 Sqn
R7	776 Sqn
R8	776 Sqn
S7	804 Sqn
W4	760 Sqn
W7	760 Sqn
W8	760 Sqn
W9	760 Sqn
Y1	759 Sqn
Y2	759 Sqn
YØ	787 Sqn

Design and layout by Magali Masselin.

All rights reserved. No part of this publication can be transmitted or reproduced wihtout the written consent of all the autors and the publisher.

ISBN: 978-2-915239-87-4

Publisher's number: 915239

© Histoire & Collections 2010

5, avenue de la République
F-75541 Paris Cédex 11
FRANCE

Tel: +33-1 40 21 18 20 / Fax: +33-1 47 00 51 11
www.histoireetcollections.com

This book has been designed, typed, laid-out and processed by *Histoire & Collections* on fully integrated computer equipment.

Color separation: *Studio A&C*

Print by *MCC GRAPHICS - ELKAR*, Spain, European Union.

October 2010